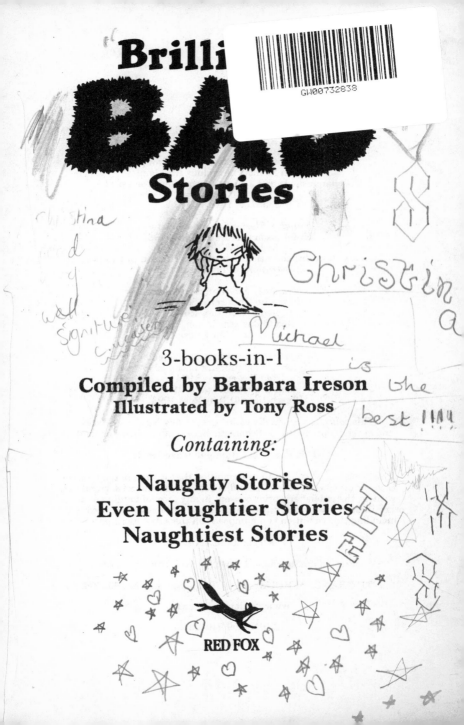

"Brilli[ant]

BAD

Stories

3-books-in-1

Compiled by Barbara Ireson
Illustrated by Tony Ross

Containing:

Naughty Stories
Even Naughtier Stories
Naughtiest Stories

RED FOX

A Red Fox Book

Published by Random House Children's Books
20 Vauxhall Bridge Road, London, SW1V 2SA

A division of The Random House Group Ltd
London Melbourne Sydney Auckland
Johannesburg and agencies throughout the world

3 5 7 9 10 8 6 4 2

Naughty Stories first published by
Hutchinson Children's Books 1989
Red Fox edition 1991
Text © in this collection Century Hutchinson Ltd 1989
Illustrations © Tony Ross 1989

Even Naughtier Stories first published by
Hutchinson Children's Books 1990
Red Fox edition 1991
Text © Barbara Ireson 1990
Illustrations © Tony Ross 1990

Naughtiest Stories first published by
Hutchinson Children's Books 1993
Red Fox edition 1994
Text © Barbara Ireson 1993
Illustrations © Tony Ross 1993

This collection originally called *Completely Naughty Stories*
and specially produced for Scholastic Book Club by Red Fox in 1995

This Red Fox edition published 1999

Printed and bound in Norway by AIT Trondheim AS

THE RANDOM HOUSE GROUP Limited Reg. No. 954009

www.randomhouse.co.uk

ISBN 0 09 940128 2

Brilliantly BAD Stories

Contents

The Boy Who Made Faces

Eileen Colwell

There was once a boy called Fred. He was not at all a nice little boy. He left his toys out in the rain, he hated washing, he pulled the cat's tail, he drew on the wallpaper, he said 'Shan't' when anyone asked him to do things.

One day he found out that he could make such ugly faces that it upset everyone who saw them. Soon he gave up his other tricks and just made faces instead. Only to look at him gave little girls bad dreams and when his friends played with him and were winning he would make such horrible faces that they were put off and lost the games. 'It's not fair!' they said and they wouldn't play with him any more. When Fred's favourite aunt came to see him he pulled such a frightful face that she never came back again but just sent a card on his birthday. The only person who didn't see him making faces was his mother – he didn't want to upset *her*. So she was surprised when

1

visitors screamed or fainted because of the horrible faces Fred was making behind her back. 'Freddie is such a kind little boy,' she said, 'and he always has a nice smile.'

Fred wouldn't listen to his friends and relations when they warned him that his face would stay that horrid shape if the wind changed. 'Pooh!' said Fred rudely, and stood out in the wind when it was changing to see what happened. But nothing did.

His father smacked him but that only made him twist his face more because it had hurt. At school he spent a lot of time in the corner looking at the wall so that the teacher couldn't see the faces he was making. She said it made her forget what she was supposed to be teaching – not that the children minded that.

It didn't matter what people said or did, Fred made faces and that was that.

One day Fred's Uncle Charles came to see him. He had been in faraway foreign countries for years and years and this was the first visit since Fred was born. Fred was very excited about his uncle's visit for he would bring a present of course – all proper aunts and uncles do – and he might know some different kinds of faces Fred could make, the kind they make in Peru or Timbuktu.

Uncle Charles did bring a present, a carved wooden monkey, which Fred thought was rather dull. Uncle Charles looked quite ordinary anyway except that he carried a walking stick everywhere and sometimes pointed it at people who annoyed him. When he did so the stick lighted up at the end with a blue crackly light and the people stopped whatever they were saying and went away very quickly. Otherwise nobody worried for they thought it was probably the odd way people behaved in the foreign countries where Uncle Charles had been living.

Sometimes, too, Uncle Charles would put his hand in his pocket and bring out some strange creature, a jerboa or a salamander perhaps. 'Oh well,' said Fred's mother, 'Charles was always interested in Nature.' Perhaps so, but Fred wondered why the salamanders and other creatures were all colours of the rainbow and why they suddenly vanished. Sometimes Fred would ask his uncle why he carried these strange

creatures in his pockets and where they went when they disappeared. 'Strange creatures in my pockets? Rubbish, boy!' said Uncle Charles. 'You can see for yourself there are none there.' And he turned his pockets inside out.

At first Fred didn't make faces at Uncle Charles because he was too interested to see what his uncle would do next and, besides, he was a little nervous of him. But one day he forgot and made a frightful face. Uncle Charles watched him with interest. 'Not bad,' he said kindly. 'Do it again.' Fred did. 'Hmm. . . .' said Uncle Charles thoughtfully.

'Would you like to enter for a competition in making faces? You might do well.'

'Oh, could I?' asked Fred, delighted. 'Where is the competition?'

'There's a fair in the town,' said Uncle Charles. 'There should be one there. Let's go, boy.'

So off they went together, Uncle Charles carrying his walking stick as usual. 'How nice to see Freddie and his uncle such good friends,' said Fred's mother.

At the fair there were all sorts of things to see – a Fat Woman, performing dogs, a very large man who could lift heavy weights marked ONE TON. There were hot-dog stalls and candy-floss stalls and several kinds of roundabouts. Fred chose to ride on one which had cars and aeroplanes, but Uncle Charles preferred a jungle roundabout and rode on a lion, his long legs dangling on either side. Fred *thought* he heard the lion roar and saw it shake its mane when Uncle Charles got on its back, but he must have been mistaken, of course.

Several times when they had to pay for seeing things or riding on things, Uncle Charles put his hand in his pocket and brought out one of the strange creatures. Fred had to remind his uncle that they wouldn't do instead of money. 'Dear me, where could those have come from?' said Uncle Charles as the salamanders and jerboas disappeared. The people at the fair watched in astonishment.

Fred wasn't very good at throwing the wooden balls at the coconut shy, but however badly he threw, he was surprised to find that he nearly always hit the coconuts. Then he noticed that when Uncle Charles pointed his stick at the balls, they turned round in the air and hit the coconuts with a bang. Fred collected a whole armful of them and the man in charge didn't like it at all. 'Clear off, guv'nor,' he said crossly. 'It ain't fair!'

So Uncle Charles gave him all the coconuts back except one for Fred to take home.

Then they came to a large tent which had a poster outside – COMPETITIONS. TRY YOUR LUCK. Fred and his uncle paid their money and went in. In a dark corner sat an old man with a rubbery kind of face. He was saying in a tired, hoarse voice, 'Make faces and win a bicycle!' over and over again.

'Ha! Now's your chance, boy,' said Uncle Charles.

Fred went up to the old man and so did three other children. 'Wot you does,' said the old man, 'is to stand on this 'ere platform and make as many different horrid faces as you can, see. The one that makes the most faces and keeps it up longest wins the bicycle.'

The first boy was so nervous that, instead of making horrid faces, he looked quite pleasant and gave up almost at once. The next entrant, a girl, did so well that the old man told her to wait. The third to enter was Fred.

'Now, Fred, do your best. Don't let me down,' said Uncle Charles.

Fred began. He made face after face while Uncle Charles looked on approvingly.

Fred went on, changing expressions as fast as he could. At first he enjoyed it, but soon his face began to get tired. 'Isn't that enough?' he asked, but the old man didn't answer but only stared at him with his mouth open like a fish.

'Keep it up, boy,' said Uncle Charles, clapping loudly.

Now Fred was making such horrible faces and so fast that he even frightened himself when he caught sight of his face in the mirror on the canvas walls.

'Can't I stop now?' he asked imploringly.

'Don't you want to win?' said his uncle. 'Come, come, get on with it.'

On and on went Fred until his face ached all over. 'Do let me stop!' he begged.

'Faster, *faster*, FASTER!' said his uncle relentlessly – and Fred burst into tears. 'I can't bear it any longer,' he sobbed.

'STOP!' exclaimed Uncle Charles and he pointed his stick at Fred and the old man. A blue light crackled and Fred found himself at his uncle's side. His face had stopped moving and it felt stiff all over.

'Next!' said the old man hoarsely.

'I want to go home,' said Fred, sniffing.

'But you might win the prize! The other boy may not do as well as you did.'

'I don't care what he does,' said Fred. 'Let's go

home *please*.'

'Better luck next time,' said Uncle Charles. 'You'll improve with practice.'

'I don't want to practise. I don't want to make faces ever again,' said Fred.

Next morning Uncle Charles had gone before Fred woke up. Fred still felt he didn't want to make faces. He went to school and the teacher didn't put him in the corner once and the other boys seemed quite friendly, although Fred couldn't think why they had changed.

One morning Fred looked in the mirror and saw a boy he didn't recognize, a boy with a cheerful expression and a nice, friendly smile. It was himself! And behind him he saw Uncle Charles; and his uncle was smiling too. The next moment there was no one there. How could there be!

A few days afterwards, a large packing case arrived addressed to Fred. Inside was a marvellous bicycle with all the extra gadgets Fred had longed for. The carved wooden monkey Uncle Charles had given him made a splendid mascot for the handlebars.

'Now, whoever could have sent this to you, darling?' asked his mother. Fred was sure it was Uncle Charles but he never said so to anyone for, after all, Uncle Charles was in a faraway country and couldn't possibly know that Fred had stopped making faces. Or could he, perhaps?

Isabelle the Itch

Constance C. Greene

When she got home, Isabelle stomped out to the kitchen. It was empty so she stomped upstairs. Her mother was looking at herself in the mirror critically.

'They say lines lend character to a face,' she said moodily. 'If that's true, I must have some character.'

'Why can't I have a pyjama party tonight?' Isabelle whined.

'Because your father and I are going to a party, that's why.'

'So what?' Isabelle sprawled on her mother's bed, messing up the bed-spread. 'We could take care of ourselves.'

Her mother looked at her. 'Some days I'm too old to be a mother and today's one of them.'

'Some days you look too old and some days you look too young,' Isabelle told her. 'This is one of your old days.'

'Thanks, that makes me feel a lot better.'
Isabelle's mother got a long dress out of her
wardrobe and held it up against herself. 'They say
if you never throw anything out, eventually it'll
come back into fashion,' she said. 'Wasn't I smart
to hang on to this?'

'Who's baby-sitting?' Isabelle grumbled.

Her mother put blue stuff on her eyelids and
drew a mouth over her own with a new lipstick.
'Mrs Oliver has a virus so I guess Philip will have
to be in charge. We're only going a couple of
blocks away and I'll leave the number.'

Isabelle hurled herself on the floor and kicked
at the rug. 'I won't stay with him,' she stormed.
'He's a big boss when he's in charge. He bosses
me around something terrible. I'll run away.'

She stomped into her room and started
throwing things around. She threw her favourite
copy of the *Wizard of Oz* into a corner, then she
opened her wardrobe door and threw her shoes

and rubber boots out and started cleaning the wardrobe floor with her shirt-tail.

'I bet the neighbours would be shocked if they saw the dirt in this house. That wardrobe hasn't been cleaned in a month of Sunday's,' she said at the top of her voice.

Isabelle's mother was sensitive about her house cleaning. She wasn't too good at it. Nothing drove her crazy faster than people who said they just didn't know what was the matter, but they couldn't stand a less-than-immaculate house. Isabelle's mother always said there were lots more important things in this world than a kitchen floor you can eat off.

When she ran out of nasty things to say, Isabelle went to the kitchen and stuck her finger into the jar of peanut butter as far as it would go.

ISABELLE WAS HERE, she wrote in peanut butter on the fridge door.

Her father stood in the doorway.

'Get a sponge and wipe that off,' he directed.

Isabelle scrubbed off the peanut butter while he watched. For good measure, she scrubbed out the kitchen sink. Hard, as hard as she could, she scrubbed until it shone.

Her father inspected her work.

'When you set your mind to it, you can do a first-class job,' he told her. He put his hand on the top of her head, something he did only when he was pleased with her. Isabelle stood very still, enjoying the warm weight of it.

'I'll tell you one thing, Isabelle. When you make up your mind to do something, you can do it. Someday you're going to scale mountains,' he said softly. 'When you stop trying to beat the world single-handed, things will fall into place for you.' He hugged her. She smelled the scent of his clothes with delight and thought he was right.

'Mum said I can't have a pyjama party,' she said.

'Is that one of those affairs where you don't close your eyes all night?' he asked.

Her mother twirled in front of them, showing off her dress and dangly earrings.

'You going some place?' her father asked.

'The Gwynnes. I told you last week.'

'Look how I cleaned the sink for you, Mum,' Isabelle said.

'Terrific. It hasn't looked that clean for weeks.'

'I don't want to go to the Gwynnes,' Isabelle's father said. 'They bore me.'

'You get to have all the fun,' Isabelle went upstairs and looked up Mary Eliza's number.

'Shook residence, Mary Eliza speaking,' a voice said.

'Let me speak to Mary Eliza Shook please,' Isabelle said.

Silence. 'This *is* Mary Eliza,' the voice said in an irritated way.

Isabelle made a very loud, very rude noise into the receiver and hung up.

She went back to the kitchen.

'You have a choice.' Her mother took two TV dinners out of the freezer. 'Salisbury steak or meat loaf.'

'You'd better tell Philip not to hit me,' Isabelle said. 'The last time you left him in charge, he ate all the ice cream, plus a jar of apple sauce, and he put his feet on the couch. *And* he said I had to go to bed at nine but he stayed up until he heard the car coming.'

'How do you know?' her mother asked.

'I spied on him. He called up his friends and swore at them over the telephone too.'

'Maybe I'd better stay home to see that law and order prevails,' her father said.

'What if I get a pain in my stomach or a

toothache? Philip wouldn't know what to do and I might even die.' Isabelle could feel the tears start.

'I'll speak to him before we go,' her father said.

Isabelle went to her room and threw a few more things around until she heard Philip come home.

'What do you want?' she said, going down to the kitchen and taking the two TV dinners out of the freezer.

'I'll take the Salisbury steak,' he said.

'No you won't. I want it. Mum said I get first choice.'

'That's OK, monster, you made me lose my appetite anyway,' he said.

After her parents had left for the party, Isabelle put on her swimming mask and flippers and filled the bath with water so hot that it left a red mark on her as far as it reached. She lay face down in the water looking at the bottom of the bath. No man-eating fish there. She kicked as hard as she could, escaping from the mysterious blue whale. When she surfaced, she was gratified to see the amount of water covering the bathroom floor. The ends of her fingers were puckered. She wouldn't have to take another bath for a month, she was so clean.

Isabelle put on her dressing gown and pyjamas and ate her Salisbury steak. It was tough. The peas and carrots tasted green and orange. The mashed potatoes didn't taste at all. She threw half

the dinner away, then went upstairs to get a sock out of her drawer. Placing it over the telephone receiver to disguise her voice, she made another telephone call.

'Hello,' a man's voice answered at Sally Smith's house.

'This is Sgt Brown down at the police station,' Isabelle said through the sock. 'We have complaints that you're making too much noise at your house. We might have to send a squad car over if you don't stop all the yelling.'

She hung up and made hideous faces at herself in the mirror.

PHILIP IS A FINK, she wrote in huge letters on her blackboard. Wet hair streaming on either side of her face, she lay down on her bed and, before she could stop herself, fell asleep.

Trouble with the Fiend

Sheila Lavelle

It takes some doing to play a trick on the whole class at the same time, but Angela managed to think of a way. And of course once again it was me that got the blame.

She worked herself up in a right old temper that day, and it was only because everybody laughed at her during the art lesson. Angela hates art anyway, and Miss March is always telling her off for messy, untidy work.

It was an interesting sort of lesson, because for a change we weren't doing painting. We were learning how to do that old-fashioned italic writing. And we all had those special pens with thick nibs and little bottles of black Indian ink.

We had to copy a poem from the blackboard, and I was quite enjoying making the nice curved shapes of the letters and putting fancy squiggly bits on the capitals. I only made one or two small blots, and on the whole I thought my effort wasn't too bad.

Angela, in the desk behind mine, wasn't getting on at all well. Everybody was working away quietly, with Miss March walking around the class looking over our shoulders and helping here and there, so we could all hear Angela sighing and moaning and screwing up her sheet of paper to start again.

'This is murder,' she hissed in my ear. 'This lousy pen doesn't work. It keeps making blobs.'

'Try a new nib,' I whispered, starting on the last line of the verse.

Angela clattered out to the front of the class to change her nib from the box on the shelf. When she got back to her place with a fresh piece of paper she found Miss March looming over her like a mountain.

'Angela Mitchell,' said Miss March grimly. 'I can't believe you haven't even started yet. Your paper's still blank. What have you been doing all this time?'

'She's been writing blank verse, Miss,' said that cleverclogs Laurence Parker. 'Like Shakespeare.' And you should have heard the groans from the rest of the class.

'You've only got five minutes left, Angela,' went on Miss March coldly, ignoring Laurence's remark. 'If it's not finished by the end of the lesson you'll have to stay in after lunch. Now please get on with it.'

I hoped Miss March might say something nice about my work on the way past, but she only gave it a quick glance and a nod and walked on. I finished the poem and put a neat little row of dots at the bottom. I blotted the ink carefully with a clean piece of blotting paper, then I looked over my shoulder at Angela.

She was scribbling away like a maniac, her face all red and her fingers smudged with ink. Her paper was a mess, all covered in splashes and dribbles and blotches, and she kept jabbing the pen furiously into the ink bottle as if she was trying to stab it to death.

The bell went for lunch and Angela finished just in time. She slumped back in her seat and flung down the pen with a huge sigh.

Miss March came to have a look. She picked up Angela's paper and glared at it in silence for a while. Angela didn't even look at her. She sank down in her chair, her eyes fixed on the desk.

'A five-year-old could have done better than this,' said Miss March finally in a grim sort of voice. 'It looks as if ten drunken spiders fell in the ink and crawled all over the page.' And of course that's when the whole class fell about laughing. Not because it was all that funny, but because it was a teacher's joke.

Laurence Parker got the job of collecting all the

papers and everybody else trooped out down the corridor.

'Never mind,' I said to Angela, giving her arm a squeeze. 'At least Miss Quick March didn't keep you in.' Angela was hardly listening. She had a very funny look in her eyes.

'They didn't have to laugh at me like that,' she said moodily. 'I'll think of a way to get even with the whole stupid lot of them. You'll see.'

And all the time we were eating our school dinner in the dining hall Angela sat like a statue staring into space. She hardly ate any of her stew and carrots and mashed potatoes, or her apple crumble and custard, much to the delight of Laurence Parker, who scoffed the lot.

When we were on our way out into the playground after lunch Angela grabbed me by the arm.

'Charlie,' she said, and my heart sank when I saw the gleeful expression on her face. 'I've had a fabulous idea.'

She dragged me along the corridor towards the changing rooms at the end. There was nobody around at this hour as they were all outside. Angela shoved me down on the bench beside the girls' lockers and sat beside me.

'What's first lesson this afternoon?' she said, making her eyes go all narrow.

'Games,' I said at once. 'It's Tuesday, isn't it? It's games all afternoon.'

'Right,' said Angela. 'And what will happen if we take half an hour to get changed?'

'Miss March will do her nut,' I said. 'She only gives us sixty seconds, and then she blows that stupid whistle.' I looked into Angela's face, hoping for some sort of a clue. 'What are you up to?' I said.

Angela gave me a quick hug. 'You and me, Charlie, are going to cause chaos this afternoon. We're going to mix up all the games kits, so that everybody ends up with the wrong shorts and T-shirts and stuff. Can you imagine what it'll be like? It'll be a right old shambles.'

I could imagine it very clearly and I was horrified at the thought. I stood up quickly and started to argue. But Angela pushed me down again firmly.

'You're not going to say you won't help me, are you?' she said, hands on hips. 'Because if you are I'm never going to be your friend again. So you can make up your mind, Charlie Ellis.' And she started pulling shorts and T-shirts and plimsolls out of people's lockers and muddling them up in a heap on the floor.

And do you know, for once in my life it didn't take long for me to make up my mind. I sat there thinking about all the things she had ever done to get me in trouble, and all the nasty tricks she'd played on me in the past and I found it wasn't such a horrid decision, after all. I was better off without her, if only I could find the courage to tell her so.

I jumped up in a hurry before I had time to change my mind. I took a deep breath and looked her straight in the eyes.

'Well I think it's a stupid idea and it'll just cause trouble for everybody and Miss March will get mad and she's sure to keep us in until she finds out who did it and for once it's not going to be me that gets the blame because this time you can do your own dirty work. So there.'

Angela's mouth dropped open and she was giving me a real frosty-nosed stare.

'All right,' she said. 'If that's the way you want it. But you'll be sorry, Miss Hoity-toity Ellis. Don't say I didn't warn you.'

Angela started rummaging round in the lockers again and I scuttled off down the corridor as fast as I could to the playground, feeling relieved at my escape. And when I got outside I found that nice new girl Nicola Daley sitting all by herself on the wall in the sunshine. She's tall and skinny like me and she's got lovely long shiny brown hair and she's going to be a dancer when she grows up. Anyway, she gave me such a nice big smile when she saw me that I went over and sat beside her.

'Where did you live before you moved here?' I said, to start the conversation.

'Yewesly,' she told me, with a giggle. 'It's near Manchester. Funny name for a place, isn't it?'

'Not half,' I agreed. 'There was a young lady from Yewesly. . . .' But I had to stop there because I couldn't think of a rhyme.

'Who always would breakfast on muesli,' said Nicola. And we both burst out laughing.

So we sat there on the wall giggling away like anything together and making up a funny poem to send in my next letter to Uncle Barrie, and the last line was so awful I knew my Uncle Barrie would love it.

There was a young lady from Yewesly,
Who always would breakfast on muesli.
When asked for her diet,
She said 'You should try it,
It's muesli, in Yewesly, usually.'

By the time the bell went we were the best of friends, and we were enjoying ourselves so much that I'd forgotton all about Angela and her latest plot. It was only when Miss March blew her whistle in the corridor that I remembered, and my stomach suddenly rolled over as if it was full of live eels.

'You have sixty seconds to change, starting from NOW!' bellowed Miss March, and everybody rushed to their lockers and started pulling out their games kit.

'Hey, this isn't my T-shirt,' somebody called out.

'I've got the wrong shorts,' squealed somebody else.

Everybody started shrieking and yelling and fighting and snatching things from one another and chucking plimsolls around and in no time at all it was absolute pandemonium. I looked for Angela and there she was, right in the middle of the fun, giggling helplessly and shouting 'Who's got my bloomin' T-shirt?' at the top of her voice.

Well, some of them didn't half look daft, I can tell you. Angela had even mixed up some of the boys' things with ours, and she was dancing around in an enormous pair of baggy shorts that could only have belonged to Laurence Parker. That awful Delilah Jones, who is by far the tallest girl in the class, was struggling into a skimpy little T-shirt that hardly came down to her tummy button. Jane Baxter, who's really tiny, had shorts almost down to her ankles and a huge pair of plimsolls that flopped about like flippers when she tried to walk. And they were all making so much noise you could hardly hear Miss March's whistle.

'Get out here at once,' stormed Miss March from the corridor, and everybody scrambled towards the door.

I was so busy watching the others that I hadn't

even started getting changed myself. I quickly pulled off my skirt and blouse and grabbed the stuff in my locker, dreading the sight of what Angela had selected for me.

The games kit in my locker was all my own. I stared at the clothes, astonished. I checked the name labels and they all said Charlotte Ellis and I was baffled. Why hadn't Angela mixed up my things as well? I very soon found out.

Miss March was stamping her feet and blowing her whistle like mad by now and everybody had given up trying to sort out the mess and was tumbling out into the corridor. And it was even funnier out there because the boys all started to hoot with laughter when they saw the girls and the girls all screamed and giggled when they caight sight of the boys and the noise was unbelievable.

Laurence Parker was the funniest. He had struggled into the tiniest pair of shorts you ever saw and his big fat belly was sticking out at the top. He had ripped the T-shirt when putting it on and it hung in tatters from his shoulders like the Incredible Hulk's.

'SILENCE!' roared Miss March suddenly, and everybody went quiet.

'Form two lines,' she snapped, and everybody shuffled into place, the boys down one side of the corridor and the girls' line behind Nicola Daley, who had one toe in a very small plimsoll and the other foot in one that looked as if it would fit my dad.

There was a long silence while Miss March glared at us all. All you could hear was her snorting like a dragon. I expected sparks to come flying out of her nose at any minute.

Then she started walking down between the lines, inspecting everybody like a sergeant major in the army, and you could see people's knees tremble as she stopped at each one.

Finally she reached me. She looked me up and down in silence and then suddenly she grabbed me by the shoulder and peered at the name tags in the back of my T-shirt and shorts. Her mouth went into a grim line and that's when it hit me like a ton of bricks. I was the only person in the whole class wearing my own things. My dear friend Angela had done it again.

'That wasn't very clever of you, Charlotte Ellis,' grated Miss March through teeth like tombstones. 'It's perfectly clear who is responsible for this . . . this . . . *riot* this afternoon. You will all change back into your ordinary clothes at once, and we will have a free activities afternoon instead of games.' She looked at me as if I was the nastiest little creature she had ever set eyes on.

'Charlotte Ellis will stay here and sort out this mess. She will put everybody's things exactly where she found them. And there will be no more games for Miss Ellis for the rest of the term.'

My face went scarlet. I could see Angela grinning like a shark at the front of the line. I felt like punching her right in the nose, I can tell you.

'Please, Miss March,' I said quickly. 'It wasn't me. It was . . . it was. . . .'

'Well?' said Miss March, folding her arms and waiting.

But I closed my mouth tight and tears pricked the back of my eyelids. I found I couldn't tell tales, even on somebody as horrible as Angela. I suppose I'm stupid, but that's the way it is.

So everybody else had a lovely afternoon, reading library books, drawing and painting, and working at hobbies like sewing and knitting and weaving and stuff. And I spent the rest of the day sorting out all the games kit. It was an awful job and it took me hours. Only one thing kept me going while I worked. I would walk home with my nice new friend Nicola Daley and tell that Angela Mitchell to go and jump in the river.

Things never work out the way you want them to. When the bell finally went I put the last pair of plimsolls thankfully into the right locker and went for my coat. And there was Nicola coming out of the cloakroom, chatting and smiling away, arm in arm with Angela.

'Walk home with us, Charlie?' invited Angela

cheerfully, offering her other arm as if nothing had happened.

'I'd rather walk home with a crocodile,' I snapped. I meant it, too, At least with a crocodile you always know whose side it's on.

Boffy and the Teacher Eater

Margaret Stuart Barry

Boffy was six years old. He was small and rather thin. Large spectacles covered his pale, serious face. Boffy did not think about tadpoles and chewing-gum and model cars the way other boys did, he wanted more than anything to be an inventor.

'You can't be one until you're grown-up,' said his tall important-looking father. 'You're not old enough.'

'But I'm a genius,' pointed out Boffy.

'Yes,' said his mother, whose name was Mrs Smith, 'I'm afraid he is.'

She found living with a genius very difficult; geniuses are inclined to think it's tea-time when it's only breakfast-time. And they make complicated arrangements with the biscuits instead of just eating them. And *always* use a long word where a short one would do.

Mr Smith was going to work. He was rushing to

31

catch the underground train. Boffy had made a wonderful vehicle out of empty fruit cans. It hopped on and off pavements, knew where not to bump into lamp-posts without being told, and could even climb over things if necessary, like a caterpillar.

'Borrow it,' suggested Boffy. 'It will get you there more quickly.'

'No, thank you,' said Mr Smith politely. He preferred the more conventional form of transport.

So Boffy climbed into the fruit-can vehicle himself, and rattled off to town to collect his mother's groceries. He loaded beans into one container, potatoes into another, and secured half a boiled pig to the back. He took longer doing this than he had expected, so when he came to the gasworks he drove straight over it instead of going round it, which saved a lot of time. This greatly surprised Constable Scuffer. But by the time he'd thought what to do about it Boffy was out of sight.

Mrs Smith was glad to have her groceries so quickly. She wanted to get lunch in the oven early so that she could make a start with her springcleaning.

Soon the kitchen was full of buckets and mops and soap and polish and dusters and dishcloths.

'Did you ever see such dust!' she exclaimed. She was red in the face and quite bothered.

'I'll help you,' said Boffy.

'No, thank you,' panted Mrs Smith; she was aghast at the thought of another of Boffy's inventions.

'There must be quicker ways of cleaning a room than this!' Boffy waved his hand at the conglomeration of mops and dusters.

'There is no better way than by getting down on one's hands and knees,' answered his mother, beginning to do just that.

But Boffy was already in his little workshop behind the cabbage patch. He knew exactly what he was going to do because, as I have told you before, he was a genius. In no time at all he had made a large interesting-looking machine. It had a horn at one end, and a plastic sack at the other, and it was held together by a great many rubber tubes.

'What is it?' asked Mrs Smith, as Boffy appeared in the kitchen doorway with the new invention.

'It's a Dust Extractor, of course.'

'Well, I don't need it.' His mother was quite firm. 'I've been doing my spring-cleaning this way for a good many years now, and I don't intend to change.'

'Yes, but look how long it takes you.' Before Mrs Smith could stop him, he had switched on the Dust Extractor.

'It works!' cheered Boffy.

I cannot describe the noise that followed – like a percussion band, but noisier! Anyway, it drowned Mrs Smith's screams of 'Stop! Stop!'

Brooms and mops rattled up into the Dust Extractor. A jar of marmalade flew off the table, followed by cups and saucers and the tablecloth. Boffy was delighted. Not *all* his inventions worked. This one was doing fine. He moved it closer to the cooker, which looked extremely dusty. At once the pans came to life. Off flew the lids and out popped the potatoes and the runner beans. They slithered and bumped down the

tubes of the Dust Extractor. They took the boiling water with them and carried on cooking merrily inside the plastic bag. Last of all the oven door swung open and out shot half a pig.

Mrs Smith was completely DISTRAUGHT.

'You are a DISGRACE!' thundered Boffy's father when he came home for lunch (which was now only a buttered biscuit and a cup of tea). 'You will go straight to your room, without lunch, without afternoon tea, and without supper, and you will *stay* there. And while you are there you will rid your head of all nonsensical ideas.'

'I'm sorry, Father,' apologized Boffy. And he polished his spectacles on his shirt.

It was hard being so awfully clever.

For a whole week Boffy behaved like a model boy – more or less. He sat in the garden and counted bees. When he had counted five hundred and sixty-nine he thought of a number and divided them by it. Then he counted earwigs and subtracted them from the number of leaves on the mulberry bush.

When the dustbin-lorry arrived he carted his Dust Extractor round to the front garden and offered it to the dustbin-men. At first they did not want to take it, but when they saw how it operated they said, 'Thank you very much. This will make our job a whole lot easier.'

And they took it away.

Mr and Mrs Smith didn't know themselves, it was so quiet around the place. Mrs Smith was worried.

'Do you think you ought to have been *quite* so severe with Boffy?' she wondered.

'Well, perhaps not,' answered her husband. 'But we can't have these frightful inventions of his upsetting the whole household.' (He was a little worried himself.)

'If he could invent something small – like a Boiled-egg Opener or a . . . or a. . . .' But Mrs Smith hadn't any more ideas.

'I'll speak to him,' decided Mr Smith quite kindly. 'Boffy,' he shouted down the garden, 'just be more careful in future, that's all.'

'Yes, Father,' answered Boffy. He was relieved.

The following day was a school day. Boffy was in Class IV – on account of his being so clever, that is. He should have been in Class I, but the teacher in that room couldn't cope with him. He was constantly correcting her, and she didn't like that at all. Mr Grim, however, had been to university, so he knew one or two things Boffy didn't.

Today he was in a bad mood, because it was the first day back after a holiday. He stared at the class ferociously and made Jenny Jenny cry. He threw a new piece of chalk at Herbert Entwhistle, and made them all write lines.

'He's horrible, HORRIBLE,' wept Jenny Jenny.

'Don't cry, Jenny Jenny,' comforted Boffy. 'I have an idea. Tomorrow you will have nothing to worry about.'

After tea he retired to his shed behind the cabbage patch and he thought, and he banged and he screwed and he fixed. Then he locked up, kissed his parents good night, and went to bed early. His small head was quite worn out.

Next morning Boffy collected his new invention from the shed and set off to school. He carried it a long way round down the back streets, just in case he should meet any of his important-looking father's important-looking friends. But he met the milkman, and Mr Leggit, the postman, and that was all.

The school cloakroom was packed with children when Boffy appeared in the doorway with his latest invention.

'Oooh, what's that?' asked the children, gathering round.

'It's a Teacher Eater,' explained Boffy.

'Do you mean it actually *eats* teachers?' asked the incredulous children.

'Of course it does,' replied Boffy. 'That's what I've just told you.'

The Teacher Eater was very large. It was a cross between a robot and a dragon. It was constructed chiefly of tin and had a huge jagged

37

jaw like the blade of a saw. On its face, which was simply enormous, Boffy had painted a big pleasant smile. This was not strictly necessary to the functioning of the machine, but Boffy did not want to frighten Jenny Jenny. He had even troubled to glue a black wig on to the Teacher Eater's head.

'Oooh, I like him!' said Jenny Jenny. 'He's *super*, Boffy!'

Boffy kept the Teacher Eater hidden under a pile of coats until after play, and then he wheeled it out into Class I. The Teacher Eater trundled across the classroom floor and completely devoured the Infants' teacher.

'Hurray!' cheered the children.

The uproar brought the other teachers racing out of their rooms. They clapped their hands and shouted angry commands. The Teacher Eater didn't like that; it trundled more quickly towards them. A crowd of children skipped and jumped behind it. Suddenly it fancied the Art teacher. She was a delectable mouthful. Her scarlet stockings were the last the children saw of her.

'*Mon dieu!*' gasped the French master. He had no time to say any more.

The terrible machine rolled down the corridor hungry for more. It found the Mathematics teacher rather difficult to digest: numbers and question marks shot out of its ears all over the place.

The Teacher Eater was thoroughly enjoying eating teachers. It charged hither and thither gulping them down whole until at last there was not a single one left.

Boffy stored his invention in the games cupboard and locked the door.

'Well, children,' commanded Boffy, 'back to your classrooms, and I shall be round presently.'

No one contradicted. They did as they were told. They were quite content to look upon Boffy as their new Headmaster.

Boffy retired to the Headmaster's room to draw up a new timetable. It consisted chiefly of games and do-as-you-like lessons. The children played games until they were exhausted. In the do-as-you-like lessons most of them went home.

It was not long before every parent was frantically phoning every other parent. The whole town was ringing and buzzing. Mr and Mrs Smith were thoroughly alarmed and more than a little annoyed with their son.

'You are a DISGRACE!' (again) thundered Mr Smith, 'and you will go straight to your room, without tea, without supper, and without breakfast, and you will *stay* there. And whilst you are there you will consider the damage you have done.'

The school governors sat up very late that night discussing hard and partaking of refreshments.

They were very annoyed indeed. The sort of problems they were used to dealing with were problems like whether to buy a heated fish tank, or whether to buy new desks for the Infants. They had never had to deal with a problem like the Teacher Eater. It was all extremely irritating. They decided to visit the school at nine o'clock sharp the following morning. Five minutes later they decided that they wouldn't, as the machine which ate teachers might very well turn out to be a School Governor Eater too!

'Highly probable,' they muttered wisely.

The next day all the children were in school very early. They wanted to see what Boffy had in store for them. They expected that the morning would be spent in playing games, and the afternoon in painting or in general messing around. But Boffy had been considering the matter. He was enjoying being a Headmaster, and he had decided that his pupils should get down to some serious work. He pinned up a large notice in the hall. It read:

1st lesson –   Maths
2nd lesson –   Greek
3rd lesson –   Chemistry
4th lesson –   Lecture in the assembly hall on
                'The Origin of the Species',
                given by Boffy:
                      (signed) Boffy (*Headmaster*)

'What about play-time?' complained Simon Goodbody halfway through the morning.

'You had enough play yesterday,' scolded Boffy sternly.

'But *you're* not working,' persisted Simon sulkily. 'You're just sitting in the Headmaster's room doing nothing.'

'Of course. That's what Headmasters *do*. You will stay in after school and write "I must not be bold" one hundred times.'

Simon hated that. But Boffy sounded so much like a real Headmaster that he was afraid to disobey.

Then a CATASTROPHE happened . . . the Dinner Lady did not appear. She had heard all about the dreadful Teacher Eater and was terrified out of her wits. She was afraid it might turn nasty and become a Dinner Lady Eater too. And so the children had no dinner. Jenny Jenny began to cry.

'I'm hungry, Boffy,' she wailed. 'Ever so hungry.'

'So am I,' said Johnny and Kate the twins. And they began to cry also.

Soon the whole school was wailing and moaning.

'And your lessons are too hard,' gulped Jenny Jenny, quite heartbroken, 'and I can't do them.'

'Neither can I,' sobbed all the others together.

'I wish our teacher was back,' sniffed Jenny Jenny, 'I wish he *was*.'

Boffy was cross (and worried and a bit sorry).

'One just can't please some folks,' he grunted.

At that moment, the school door opened and in stamped Mr Smith looking specially important.

'Now then! Now then!' he bellowed. 'This nonsense has gone on quite long enough. Where is the Teacher Eater, Boffy?'

Obediently Boffy unlocked the games cupboard, and there was the Teacher Eater, gleaming in the electric light.

'Right,' said Mr Smith, pulling it out. 'Now *I* have brought along an invention. It's not a new one, and it's not a big one, but it works. Your mother lent it to me.'

It was a tin opener. Mr Smith started to use it and cut a large hole in the Teacher Eater's back.

Out rolled the Infants' teacher, then the Art mistress followed closely by the Maths master, the French master, and one or two others, and finally the Headmaster himself. They sat in a heap on the floor, looking very dazed and very crumpled. They could not think where they had been or why. Then they caught sight of the Teacher Eater and remembered. The Headmaster turned very pale indeed, then he said, 'There will be a half-day's holiday today. Good afternoon children.'

When Mr Smith had driven his son home he said, 'You are a DISGRACE! (third time) and you will go straight to your room –'

'– without tea, without supper, and without breakfast,' finished Boffy for him. 'And I will consider the damage I have done, and I will *never* invent anything again – not until I'm grown-up anyway.'

Then Mr Smith laughed very loudly, and Mrs Smith laughed too. And they thought how lucky they were after all to have a genius in the family.

And all the other mothers and fathers in the town thought how lucky *they* were that they hadn't.

Friends and Brothers

Dick King-Smith

'You say that word just once more,' said William to Charlie, 'and I'll hit you.'

Charlie said it.

William hit him.

Charlie then let out a screech and kicked William on the shin, and William bellowed.

William and Charlie's mother came rushing in like a whirlwind, with a face like thunder.

'You two will drive me mad!' she stormed. 'All you do is fight, all day long!'

'William hit me,' said Charlie.

'Why did you hit him, William?'

'Because Charlie keeps on saying the same word. Whatever I say, he says the same word, over and over again. Anyway, he kicked me.'

'Will hit me first,' said Charlie.

'William,' said mother, 'you are not to hit Charlie. He is younger than you and much smaller. The next time you do, I shall hit you.'

'You didn't ought to, Mum,' said William.

'Why not?'

'I'm younger than you and much smaller.'

'Absolutely,' said Charlie.

'There you are!' shouted William madly. 'That's the word! Whatever I say, he just says "Absolutely". He doesn't even know what it means.'

'Absolutely,' said Charlie.

William let out a yell of rage and rushed at his brother with his fists clenched. Charlie dodged behind his mother, who held a furious William at arm's length.

'Now *stop* it, the pair of you!' she said.

'William, you stop attacking Charlie, and Charlie, you stop annoying Will. I cannot stand one more minute of being shut in this house with you two. Get your bikes. We'll go to the Park.'

William stumped off, limping slightly from the kick, and shouting angrily 'It's not fair!'

From behind his mother's back, Charlie's face appeared. Silently he mouthed the word 'Absolutely'.

In the Park, William rode his BMX at top speed. He felt the need to be all by himself, miles from anybody. The roads in the Park were full of steep switchback slopes, and William swooped down them flat out. Like a lot of elder brothers, he felt he had had a raw deal.

Charlie, meanwhile, was trying to see how slowly he could pedal without falling off. He had not long inherited William's old bike and was fascinated by the problems of balance. This was much more fun than a tricycle. Like a lot of younger brothers, he had forgotten all about the recent row, and was singing happily to himself. Then he came to the top of one of the steepest slopes. He grinned, and bent low over the handlebars.

His mother, walking some way behind, saw the small figure disappear from view. A moment later, a dreadful wailing started her running hard.

Halfway down the slope, Charlie lay sprawled in the road, the old bike beside him, one wheel still spinning. His face, she saw when she reached him, was covered in blood. There was a deep cut across his forehead and a set of scratches, gravel-studded, down one cheek.

At that moment William came flying back down the reverse slope and skidded to a halt, wide-eyed with horror at the scene.

'What happened?' he said miserably.

'I don't know. He must have touched the brakes and gone straight over the handlebars. Listen carefully, Will. We must get him to hospital quickly – that cut's going to need stitches. I'm going to carry him to the nearest Park gate, that one over there, and try and stop a

car to give us a lift. Can you wheel both bikes and stick them out of sight in those bushes, and then run and catch me up?'

'Yes, Mum,' said William.

He looked at his brother's face. Charlie was still crying, but quietly now.

'He'll be all right, won't he?' William said.

Twenty-four hours later Charlie, recovered now from the shock of his accident, was jabbering away nineteen to the dozen.

He remembered little of the actual crash, or of his treatment in hospital, the stitching of the cut, and the cleaning-up of his gravelly face. It was very swollen now so that one side of him didn't look like Charlie at all, but his voice was as loud and piercing as ever as he plied his brother with endless questions.

'Did you see me come off, Will?'

'No.'

'I went right over the handlebars, didn't I?'

'Suppose so.'

'How fast d'you think I was going, Will?'

'I don't know.'

'A hundred miles an hour, d'you think?' squeaked Charlie excitedly.

'I expect so, Charles,' said William in a kindly voice. 'You looked an awful mess when I got there.'

'Lots of blood, Will?'

'Yes. Ugh, it was horrible.'

'Then what happened?'

'Well, Mum ran all the way to the nearest gate carrying you, and a kind lady in a car stopped and gave us all a lift to the hospital.'

'And then they stitched me up!' said Charlie proudly.

'Yes.'

'Did you see them stitching me up, Will?'

'No, Charles.'

'I expect it was a huge great needle,' said Charlie happily. 'You've never had six stitches, have you, Will?'

'No,' said William. 'You were jolly brave, Charlie,' he said. 'You can have a go on my BMX when you're better.'

'I can't reach the pedals,' Charlie said.

'Oh. Well, you can take a picture with my Instamatic if you like.'

'Can I really, Will?'

'And you can borrow my Swiss Army knife for a bit.'

'Can I really?'

'Yes,' said William. He put his hand in his pocket and pulled out a rather squidgy-looking bar of chocolate.

'And you can have half of this,' he said.

'Gosh, thanks, Will!'

William and Charlie's mother put her head round the door, wondering at the unaccustomed silence, and saw her sons sitting side by side on Charlie's bed, chewing chocolate. William actually had his arm round Charlie's shoulders.

'Look what I've got, Mum,' said Charlie with his mouth full.

'Did you give him some of yours, Will?' said his mother.

'Naturally,' said William loftily. 'We're friends and brothers.'

Another day went by, and Charlie was definitely better. His face was much less swollen, his spirits high, his voice shriller yet.

He had made up a song about his exploits, which he sang, endlessly and very loudly.

'Who came rushing down the hill?
Charlie boy!
Who had such an awful spill?
Charlie boy!
Who came down with a terrible thud,
Covered in mud and covered in blood?
Charlie, Charlie, Charlie boy!'

William, as he occasionally did, had an attack of earache, painful enough without Charlie's singing.

'Charles,' he said as the friend and brother was

just about to come rushing down the hill for the twentieth time, 'd'you think you could keep a bit quiet?'

'Why?' shouted Charlie at the top of his voice.

'Because I've got earache.'

'Oh,' said Charlie in a whisper. 'Oh, sorry, Will. Does it hurt a lot?'

'Yes,' said William, white-faced, 'it does.'

For the rest of the day Charlie tiptoed about the house, occasionally asking William if he needed anything, and, if he did, fetching it. He guarded his brother's peace and quiet fiercely, frowning angrily at his mother when she dropped a saucepan on the kitchen floor.

'Hullo, Charlie boy!' shouted his father on his return from work, 'How's the poor old face?'

'Don't make such a noise, Dad!' hissed Charlie furiously. 'Will's got earache.'

It was now a week since Charlie's accident, a week of harmony and brotherly love.

Charlie's face was now miles better and William's earache quite gone.

They were drawing pictures, at the kitchen table, with felt pens.

'Charles,' said William. 'Can I borrow your red? Mine's run out.'

'No,' said Charlie.

'Why not? You're not using it.'

'Yes, I am,' said Charlie, picking up his red felt and colouring with it.

'You just did that to be annoying,' said William angrily.

The word 'annoying' rang a bell with Charlie, and he grinned and nodded and said 'Absolutely!'

'Charlie!' said William between his teeth. 'Don't start that again or I'll hit you!'

'You can't,' said Charlie. 'I've got a bad face.'

'I'll hit you all the same,' said William.

'I'll shout in your bad ear,' said Charlie, 'and d'you know what I'll shout?'

'What?'

'ABSOLUTELY!!' yelled Charlie and scuttled out of the room with William in hot pursuit, as life returned to normal.

Cheese, Peas and Chocolate Pudding

Betty Van Witsen

There was once a little boy who ate cheese, peas and chocolate pudding. Cheese, peas and chocolate pudding. Cheese, peas and chocolate pudding. Every day the same old things: cheese, peas and chocolate pudding.

For breakfast he would have some cheese. Any kind. Cream cheese, American cheese, Swiss cheese, Dutch cheese, Italian cheese, blue cheese, green cheese, yellow cheese, brick cheese. Just cheese for breakfast.

For lunch he ate peas. Green or yellow peas. Frozen peas, canned peas, dried peas, split peas, black-eyed peas. No potatoes, though – just peas for lunch.

And for supper he would have cheese and peas. And chocolate pudding. Cheese, peas and chocolate pudding. Cheese, peas and chocolate pudding. Every day the same old things: cheese, peas and chocolate pudding.

Once his mother bought a lamb chop for him. She cooked it in a little frying pan on the stove, and she put some salt on it, and gave it to the little boy on a little blue dish. The boy looked at it. He smelled it. (It did smell delicious!) He even touched it. But . . .

'Is this cheese?' he asked.

'It's a lamb chop, darling,' said his mother.

The boy shook his head. 'Cheese!' he said. So his mother ate the lamb chop herself, and the boy had some cottage cheese.

One day his big brother was chewing a raw carrot. It sounded so good, the little boy reached his hand out for a bite.

'Sure!' said his brother. 'Here!' The little boy

almost put the carrot in his mouth, but at the last minute he remembered, and he said, 'Is this peas?'

'No, fella, it's a carrot,' said his brother.

'Peas,' said the little boy firmly, handing the carrot back.

Once his daddy was eating a big dish of raspberry jelly. It looked so shiny red and cool, the little boy came over and held his mouth open.

'Want a taste?' asked his daddy. The little boy looked and looked at the jelly. He almost looked it off the dish. But: 'Is it chocolate pudding?' he asked.

'No, son, it's jelly,' said his daddy.

So the little boy frowned and backed away. 'Chocolate pudding!' he said.

His grandma baked cookies for him. 'Nope!' said the boy.

His grandpa bought him an ice cream cone. The little boy just shook his head.

His aunt and uncle invited him for a fried-chicken dinner. Everybody ate fried chicken and more fried chicken. Except the little boy. And you know what he ate.

Cheese, peas and chocolate pudding. Cheese, peas and chocolate pudding. Every day the same old things: cheese, peas and chocolate pudding.

But one day – ah, one day, a very funny thing

happened. The little boy was playing puppy. He lay on the floor and growled and barked and rolled over. He crept to the table where his big brother was having lunch.

'Arf-arf!' he barked.

'Good doggie!' said his brother, patting his head. The little boy lay down on his back on the floor and barked again.

But at that minute, his big brother dropped a piece of *something* from his plate. And the little boy's mouth was just ready to say 'Arf!' And what do you think happened?

Something dropped into the little boy's mouth. He sat up in surprise. Because *something* was on his tongue. And *something* was warm and juicy and delicious!

And it didn't taste like cheese. And it did *not* taste like peas. And it certainly wasn't chocolate pudding.

The little boy chewed slowly. Each chew tasted better than the last. He swallowed *something* and opened his mouth again. Wide. As wide as he could.

'Want some more?' asked his brother.

The little boy closed his mouth and thought. 'That's not cheese,' he said.

'No, it's not,' said his brother.

'And it isn't peas.'

'No, not peas,' said his brother.

'And it couldn't be chocolate pudding.'

'No, it certainly is not chocolate pudding,' smiled his brother. 'It's hamburger.'

The little boy thought hard. 'I like hamburger,' he said.

So his big brother shared the rest of his hamburger with the little boy, and ever after that, guess what!

Ever after that, the little boy ate cheese, peas, and chocolate pudding and hamburger.

Until he was your age, of course. When he was your age, he ate everything.

The Tidying Up of Thomas

Charlotte Hough

Are you a rough, untidy child? I hope not. I
expect you are very neat and clean and careful
but, well, anyway, whatever you are you just
couldn't be as bad as Thomas was because he was
worse than any other boy in the whole of England.
It was such a pity, because he was really very
lucky. Neat clean careful people like you could
have done with some of his toys, and those poor
toys could have done with you! Thomas had a
great many kind uncles and aunts with no
children and plenty of money. They had given
him a Noah's ark and a farm and a zoo and
soldiers and cars and games and paints and books
and goldfish and a rocking-horse and a blackboard and a Red Indian costume and – oh,
everything you have ever wanted. And he had a
lovely big nursery to keep them all in, with a shiny
green floor.

But he was so *rough*, and so *untidy*!

His poor mother was distracted. She didn't know what to do about Thomas.

One day he fetched the scissors out of her workbox and tried to take out his big bear's appendix. He pulled out all the stuffing and made such a mess of him that poor old Teddy would have had to be *thrown away* if Thomas's mother hadn't relented and collected it all up with a dustpan and brush and sewn him up again.

'You're a very naughty, wasteful, silly little boy!' she scolded him, 'and you don't deserve all those lovely toys. Tomorrow you shan't play in the nursery at all!'

So the next day Thomas had to play in the kitchen while his mother was writing letters, and when she went in to make the tea she found he had mixed up the sugar and the flour and the barley and the tea and he had broken the coffee-pot and spilt the vinegar. 'Oh, Thomas, Thomas!' she cried, 'I only hope you're ashamed of yourself!'

But Thomas wasn't ashamed of himself, not in the least bit! He thought he was really very clever.

He put the blackboard chalks in the pencil sharpener and made coloured powder and used it for gunpowder to make indoor fireworks with, but that didn't go right, so he left all the firework things in a heap on the floor and scribbled on the faces of the people in his books. He took the tyres off the cars and mixed them all up with the

cowboys and Indians, and oh, so many naughty
things you would hardly believe it. Not things
that you would *ever* do!

Of course somebody as naughty as Thomas
never goes to bed without making a terrible fuss
and to-do about it. First he would refuse to go at
all, and after his bath he always had to be sent
back to the bathroom because he hadn't washed
his ears, and then back again because he hadn't
cleaned out the bath. He had always either
broken his comb or lost his toothbrush or torn his
pyjamas. By the time he was really and truly in

bed and asleep his parents felt absolutely exhausted.

'We shall really have to do something about that boy,' said Thomas's father.

'Oh yes, I quite agree, we shall really *have* to,' said his mother, 'but what? We've tried smacking him, and stopping his sweets, and reasoning with him, and . . . and praising him when he's good, only he's never good, so *that* didn't work. We've tried everything.'

Meanwhile in the darkened nursery all the toys were waking up and cautiously feeling their bruises and sorting themselves out. What a rustling and whispering there was! The farmer was collecting up his flock of sheep from amongst the bricks, while Mr Noah and the zoo-keeper tried to track down *their* animals, and a toy soldier climbed stiffly out of the goldfish bowl, shaking the water out of his busby. A squeaky trumpeting came from under the bookcase, where the little zoo elephant had got pinned under a battered police-car. Luckily his friend the woolly elephant was able to pull him free and help him back to the broken cardboard box which was shared by the zoo with various paperclips, lumps of plasticine, and other odds and ends.

'We shall really have to do something about that boy,' said the kangaroo, as she searched for her baby amongst the dressing-up clothes (she eventually found him in the paintbox).

'Oh yes, I quite agree, we really *have* to,' said the woolly snake, 'but what? I can't do much to help. I've completely lost one eye and my head's getting all loose because he always picks me up by it though I distinctly heard them telling him not to.'

'You're lucky,' said a tin bus bitterly. 'Do you know, he used me instead of a hammer the other day? I've hardly got any paint left and I used to be such a beautiful red.'

'Well, look at me,' put in the rocking-horse. 'It's shocking, it really is. No mane, no tail, no stirrups, no nothing. Wobbling-horse would be a better name for me now after all my rough treatment. I'm really getting quite dangerous.'

At this the others all nodded their heads very gravely. No toy likes to be called dangerous: it is a dreadful thing for a toy to be. But it was true that the rocking-horse's bolts were getting worn and bent and it was already quite difficult to stick on him without falling off, at a gallop. Everyone knew what happened to dangerous toys: they were thrown away just as soon as anybody suspected it, before you could say 'Dustbin!' and that was the end of them. Mr Noah glanced anxiously up at the roof of the ark, which had been wrenched half off, leaving a nail showing, and the tin bus felt the jagged bit that had been left last time Thomas had thrown him at the cat, and hit the fireplace instead.

There was a thoughtful silence, broken only by a sneeze every now and then as the poor toys breathed in the dust. For a long time the nursery had been in such a mess that it was quite impossible for anybody to clean it properly.

'Well,' said the rocking-horse at last, raising his head determinedly, 'I don't like being unkind but we really can't go on like this. There is nothing else for it. We shall have to give him back some of his own medicine.'

In the middle of the night Thomas woke up. Something was scratching him. 'Bother!' he said. 'I must have left something in my bed!' and he ferreted about and found a small tin turkey. 'That's funny!' he said, 'I don't remember playing with that up here!' And he threw it out and closed his eyes.

But Thomas couldn't go to sleep. However much he rolled over in bed he always managed to lie on something hard and spiky. In the end he got up, switched the light on, and pulled his bed to pieces. There amongst the bedclothes lay all the farm animals with their sharp little legs. There were pigs in the pillowcase, sheep in the sheets, cows in the coverlet, bulls in the blankets and hens and ducks and milking girls *everywhere*.

Thomas shook them angrily out on to the floor and then he tried to make his bed again.

Thomas wasn't good at making beds. He had an uncomfortable night.

At half past seven he was up and dressed, without anybody even calling him once, pleased to leave that horrid, cold, and lumpy heap of bedclothes. He started to get his things ready for school before breakfast so that there wouldn't be the usual awful rush. (As you know, untidy children are always in an awful rush because they never know where anything is. That's why it's *so* much better to be like you.)

Before long he went running into the kitchen to find his mother. 'Look at my nature book!' he cried indignantly, holding it up before her eyes.

'Well, it's a nasty messy-looking thing,' agreed

his mother. 'But so are all your other books.'

'But this is a *school* book!' cried Thomas. 'You can't scribble on *school* books. We aren't allowed to!'

His mother looked at it more closely. 'But you have done, dear,' she said mildly. 'With all your coloured chalks.'

'But it wasn't me that did it!' shouted Thomas, nearly in tears.

'Now, Thomas,' said his mother, putting down the milk-jug and turning to face him, 'I know you're a rough, untidy boy but at least you always used to be a truthful one. I didn't scribble on your book and neither did your father. That only leaves one person who could have, doesn't it? Now, sit down and eat your breakfast and don't let me ever hear you speak an untruth again!'

Thomas opened his mouth, and then he looked at his mother's face, which was rather unusually firm, so he changed his mind and shut it again. Silently he ate his breakfast and silently he went upstairs to the bathroom to clean his teeth.

Silently he gazed at the row of empty toothpaste tubes. Silently he fetched a bowl and a cloth and cleaned the toothpaste off the bath, the floor, the walls, the door. Somebody had been enjoying themselves. Thomas worked hard. He had a wholesome respect for his father, who seldom visited the nursery, but was shortly expected in

the bathroom in order to shave.

Ten minutes later, Thomas rushed madly into the hall to get ready for school and a moment later another loud wail reached his mother's ears. 'I can't wear *this*!'

'What's the matter now, dear?'

'There aren't any buttons on my blazer!'

'Nonsense dear, they can't all have gone, not all at once!'

'They have! Just look!'

'Good gracious! So they have!' said his mother in astonishment. 'Whatever made you do such a thing? You've cut them all off! Well, there's no time to sew them on again now. You'll just have to go as you are. Really, Thomas, I can't think what's got into you! I'll just have to hide all the scissors in the house. Every single pair. You don't seem to have any *sense*!'

'But listen!' cried Thomas desperately. 'I . . . didn't . . . do . . . it!'

'Thomas! remember what I said,' warned his mother. 'Untidiness is one thing. Untruth is another.'

'But don't you see? THE TOYS DID IT!'

'Well, dear, if the toys did it I can't say I blame them, seeing the way you treat them. Perhaps now you'll realize what it's like, being treated that way. Perhaps it will teach you a lesson!'

And do you know, it did! It was really quite amazing – everybody remarked on it. 'What a lovely nursery!' they say now when they come to tea with Thomas. 'It's so neat and clean and tidy, with everything all ready for playing with, in its proper place! How nice it is to see somebody who really appreciates his toys!' and they wish that *their* little boy or girl was as good!

It's an extra special nursery.

Some people even say the toys have extra special expressions on their faces, but that seems to be going a bit far, really, don't you think?

The Not-Very-Nice-Prince

Pamela Oldfield

Prince Ferdinand was not very nice and hardly anybody liked him. Only the Princess Eglantine could put up with his rude manners, and they would visit each other fom time to time for a game of Snakes and Ladders.

One day the Prince was driving home in the royal coach when it came to a sudden halt. An old woman was crossing the road with an ancient pram laden with firewood.

The Prince put his head out of the window and shouted at her. 'I say, old woman, move that flipping pram out of my way and look sharp about it.'

The old woman looked at him. She was very ugly indeed and in need of a good wash.

'Hang on a minute, your Highness,' she croaked. 'This nearside wheel's a bit wobbly. . . .'

Now a gentleman would have offered to help her but Prince Ferdinand was no gentleman.

'Don't bother me with your excuses,' he shouted. 'Get the flipping thing out of my way.'

Well, the ugly old woman was really a witch. She didn't like his manners and decided to teach him a lesson. She pointed at him with a long bony finger and muttered some magic words. He heard the word 'flipping' but that was all.

At once the 'flipping thing' flipped. To Ferdinand's dismay the pram rose into the air and turned right over. All the firewood fell out on to the startled horses.

They were very frightened and promptly ran

away and the coach came unhitched and rolled into the hedge. The Prince climbed out of his wrecked coach and looked for the old woman but she had disappeared. He didn't know that she had put a spell on him.

But the next day a girl came to the door with a basket of eggs.

'Good day to your Highness,' she said politely. 'Will you buy some new-laid eggs?'

'No, I won't,' he said without even a thank you.

'But they are beautiful brown eggs,' she said.

'They may be sky-blue pink for all I care,' he said. 'Take the flipping things away.'

You can guess what happened!

The basket rose up into the air and turned over. The eggs fell on the Prince's best velvet coat and ruined it.

'Now I see it all!' he cried fearfully. 'The old woman was a witch and she has put a spell on me. I shall have to be very careful what I say from now on.'

The Not-Very-Nice-Prince walked about all next day with his hand clapped over his mouth so that he wouldn't say anything foolish ... but the next morning he forgot again. When the maid carried in his breakfast he sat up in bed and scowled.

'What on earth is that?' he asked.

'Crunchy Pops, your Highness.'

'Crunchy Pops!' he grumbled. 'I wanted eggs

and bacon. Take the flipping things – Ooh!'

Too late he realized what he'd said. The bowl of Crunchy Pops floated into the air and flipped right over. It emptied itself all over his head. Prince Ferdinand screamed with rage and the terrified maid fled into a nearby broom cupboard and wept copiously.

After that, things went from bad to worse. The Prince became very flustered and that made him even more forgetful. On Monday he flipped a royal banquet.

On Tuesday it was a market stall.

On Wednesday it was a troop of the King's best soldiers!

But he had finally gone too far.

'Get out of my sight,' roared the King, stamping his foot so hard that it hurt.

'Don't come back until the spell is lifted.'

Notices were put up warning people to keep away from the Prince and they didn't need telling twice.

So the unfortunate Ferdinand retired to a dark dungeon below the palace and wondered what he should do. He didn't tell anyone where he was and no one bothered to find out – which was very sad.

One day the Princess Eglantine visited the King for a game of croquet. She had almost won the game when she caught sight of the Prince watching them from the dungeon. Kindly, she offered to visit him for a game of Snakes and Ladders.

'How can I concentrate on Snakes and Ladders at a time like this?' he wailed. 'All I need is a flipping Princess who—'

He had done it again! Slowly the Princess rose into the air and turned over.

She came down on her bottom and everyone laughed.

The Princess was mortified. 'I shall be back when the spell is lifted and *not* before,' she told the King, and stomped off home with her nose in the air.

The question was – who could lift the spell? The only visitor to the dark dungeon was an old woman who took him bread and water each day. Prince Ferdinand was so busy feeling sorry for himself he didn't even recognize her. He had plenty of time to ponder his manners and vowed that if the spell were ever lifted he would be a reformed character.

One day the old woman, who was really the witch, came into the dungeon. She had a pail of water and a scrubbing brush and she began to scrub the floor. The Prince looked at her kindly.

'That is hard work for an old woman,' he said politely. 'Please let me help you.'

To the old woman's dismay he seized the scrubbing brush and fell to scrubbing the dungeon floor. She stared at him in horror.

'You nincompoop!' she roared. 'You numb-skull! Why do you have to be so polite? Your cursed good manners have lifted the spell – and broken my power also . . . Aah!'

And she vanished in a puff of horrid green smoke which smelled like burnt kippers.

Of course, the people were delighted. They carried Ferdinand through the streets rejoicing – all the way to the Princess Eglantine's palace. She was waiting eagerly for the Very-Nice-Prince and another game of Snakes and Ladders.

The Arguing Boy

Leila Berg

Now this is a tale of a boy who argued. And this is the way *I* tell it.

Once upon a time there was a boy. And he had nine big sisters. And because there were nine of them and only one of him, he always argued.

One day he had argued so much with his nine big sisters that he decided to seek his fortune. His mammy made him some sandwiches – jam butties, he called them – and she put them in a bag, and he tied them to a pole over his shoulder, which is what people do when they seek their fortune, and off he went.

The weather was terrible. It poured. The rain went straight down his collar, shot down his back, and came out of the bottom of his jeans. And his sandwiches turned into pudding. He walked along, squelch, squelch.

At last he came to a house. He decided to knock

at the door and ask if he could sleep there, in the dry.

'Can I sleep in your house?' he said to the lady.

'I'm afraid you can't.'

'But I'm sopping wet,' he said, starting to argue.

'I know you are, you poor wee thing,' she said. 'But I haven't got room.'

'You've got plenty of room,' he said, arguing. 'You've got a whole house.'

'I'm afraid it's full of people. Tell you what, I'll give you some hot soup to make you feel better. There's plenty of that still cooking.'

'I don't want hot soup. I want to sleep here.' He was very rude.

Just then the lady's husband put his head out of the door. 'Having trouble?' he said. 'Trying to sell you a vacuum cleaner, is he?'

'He wants to sleep here,' said the lady. 'I've told him we haven't got room.'

'I should say we have *not*,' said the man. 'We've a big party here, and people are sleeping every-where.'

'They can't be *everywhere*. There must be *some* room,' said the boy, arguing away, moving his feet on the doorstep, squelch, squelch.

'There's no room at all,' said the man. 'But I'll tell you what –' And here he started to whisper in the woman's ear.

'Oooh!' said the woman. 'He couldn't!'

'Yes I can!' said the boy. He was just arguing.

Whisper, whisper, went the man. 'Oooh! He'd be scared to death!' said the woman.

'I wouldn't!' said the boy, arguing again.

Whisper, whisper, went the man. And this time the woman said, 'Well, you can tell him. But don't blame me if the Bogey gets him.'

Then the man said to the boy, 'You see, it's like this. We've got a cottage next door.

There's nobody in it because of the little Red Bogey.'

'The little Red Bogey? What's that?'

'Oh, he's a sort of hobgoblin. Very fierce and bad-tempered. Perhaps you'd better not go in.'

'I will,' said the boy.

'I thought you would,' said the man. And he gave him the key.

Inside the cottage it was dry, but very dusty. No one had cleaned it for years because of the little Red Bogey.

The boy found a pile of firewood and lit a fire with some matches he found on the shelf. Soon it was blazing away. He took off his boots, spread his clothes on the floor to dry off, and lay down on the bed in the corner.

He was almost asleep in the flickering firelight and the steam coming up from his clothes and boots, when a voice said, 'I am coming!'

He didn't take much notice. After a moment, the voice said again, rather louder, 'I AM COMING!' He still took no notice.

But after another moment the voice fairly bawled, 'I AM COMING!'

He sat up and shouted, 'If you're coming then COME, or else shut up!'

A pile of soot fell down from the chimney. Then two dead birds who had been stuck there goodness knows how long. Then a lumpy red foot

79

reached down, then a second one, then the rest of the two lumpy legs, then a lumpy, bumpy, frumpy-looking little red man came scrambling down the bricks, and jumped right across the fire into the room.

'Well, what a shrimp!' said the boy. 'The noise you were making, I thought you were a giant at least!'

'Don't you talk to me like that!' said the little man. 'I'm the Red Bogey.'

'I don't care if you're a pink cauliflower,' said the boy.

The little man strode to the door and flung it open. Two men were standing there, one on each side, and they really *were* giants. 'We've got trouble here,' he said. 'Arguing boy. I may be needing you.'

The first one saluted. 'Just give us a call, sir.'

'We'll chop him into pieces,' said the second.

'Right,' said the little Red Bogey. 'Stay there.' And he closed the door again.

'Now are you frightened?' he said to the boy.

'Not a bit,' said the boy.

The little Red Bogey scowled at him, then strode into the kitchen. 'Follow me!' he shouted.

'Why should I?' said the boy.

'You'll be sorry if you don't,' said the little Red Bogey.

'Who says so?' said the boy.

'You'll be sorry if you don't,' said the little Red Bogey, grinding his teeth and swishing his tail, 'because I am going to show you something very interesting indeed, and you will be very sorry if you miss it.'

The boy thought a minute or two, then followed him. 'I *might* come,' he said.

The little Red Bogey pulled open a trap-door in the kitchen floor. Underneath were stairs leading to a cellar. 'Get down there!' he said.

'Why should I?' said the boy.

'You're frightened of the dark, I bet,' said the little Red Bogey.

'I am *not*!' said the boy. And he went down.

At the bottom was an enormous chest.

'Open it!' said the little Red Bogey.

'Open it yourself!' said the boy.

'Oh, you really are a nuisance,' said the little Red Bogey. 'You really make me so tired.' And he started to pull at the lid. He was very small, and the chest was very big, and the lid very heavy by the look of it. But the boy didn't help him at all.

The little Red Bogey kicked the chest, and pulled it, and shouted at the boy, 'You're as bad as I am!'

In the end, after a particularly heavy thump, the lid flew open and there was a pile of golden coins inside, flashing and glittering.

'Here! Who does that belong to?' said the boy.

'It's mine. All mine,' said the little Red Bogey.

'I don't believe you,' said the boy.

'Yes, it is!' shouted the little Red Bogey. 'But I'm giving it to you, if you'll only give me a chance. I'm giving it to you and the people next door.'

'No, you're not,' said the boy. 'Where did you get it?'

'I stole it.'

'Then give it back.'

'I can't give it back. It was hundreds of years ago. I've been trying to give it away over and over again, but everyone runs away from me.'

'Well it's nothing to do with me. I don't want it,' said the boy, and started to go up the steps again.

'It's a rule!' shouted the little Red Bogey. 'I stole it from a human being. So I've got to give it back to a human being. That's the rule!'

The boy stood still and thought, while the little Red Bogey waved his tail like an angry cat.

Then he said, 'Oh well, if there's a rule, that's different. All right, I'll take it.'

'Thank goodness for that,' said the little Red Bogey. 'Let me get away from you and have some peace.' And he dashed up the steps, and the boy came into the room just in time to see the red knobbly feet vanishing up the chimney.

'I wonder if the giants are still outside the door,' he said. But they'd gone too.

In the morning, the man and woman from next door came round to see if he was all right. They were pleased to find him still there, and very surprised to hear about the money. Very pleased too.

The boy bought four tins of paint with some of his share, and painted the cottage yellow and white so that he could live there. Later he asked their daughter to marry him, and when she said no, he argued.

But she said, 'If you argue with me, I'll never speak to you again. Ask me again next year, without arguing in between.'

And the next year she said yes.

They had twelve children, six of them boys, six of them girls. And none of them ever argued, not even about how that chestful of money had got into the cottage in the first place.

Snip snap snover
That story's over

Freddie, the Toothbrush Cheat

Wendy Craig

Freddie sat at the kitchen table collecting crumbs and arranging them in a circle around the rim of his plate. His mother was at the sink, elbow-deep in foam, washing the dishes after supper, and Freddie looked up at her feeling warm and full and sleepy. It would soon be bedtime; Freddie didn't mind going to bed too much in the winter when it was dark and cold outside and he could wriggle down in his bed like a snake with his comics and have a little read and a laugh before the light went out. But then his heart sank; he would have to have a bath and clean his teeth. Ugh.

Now Freddie was a friendly boy, very pleasant company and fun to be with, but he hated soap and water with all his heart and, even more, hated cleaning his teeth. The whole business bored and annoyed him so much that the thought of it made him want to hide from his mother, or even run away rather than have to go through with it again. He felt depressed and stuck his thumb in his mouth and gave it a good suck, at the same time twirling a strand or two of hair with his other hand. His mother had just finished putting away the last knife and fork in the drawer when she saw him from the corner of her eye.

'Come on, Freddie, you look tired, darling. It's half past eight, I'll just go and run your bath.' And she went upstairs.

Freddie let out a groan and felt himself sag. 'Here we go again,' he thought. 'All that palaver. Soap in my eyes, up my nose, in my mouth, and that awful, boring toothbrush.' He could bear it no longer and furtively climbed into the kitchen waste-bin and pulled the lid over himself. It was a bit smelly in there. They'd had kippers for tea and the bones crushed under his shoes, but it was preferable he thought to the smell of rose-pink soap. He heard his mother re-enter the kitchen. She called him, then sighed when he didn't answer. Lifting the flap of the waste-bin an inch or two, he found himself gazing at her flowery apron and he quickly shut it again, but she heard the thud and pulled him out without ceremony and chased him up the stairs whacking his bottom with the loofah.

Freddie was in a frightful rage by now; he shouted and wailed, whilst his mother soaped and scrubbed him. The flannel got in his mouth, and his ears filled with bubbles, hot angry tears dripped into the lather as he slipped and slithered in an attempt to escape his mother's grasp, but she held him firmly and didn't let him escape until he was rosy and clean, and wrapped in a warm white towel.

'Oh, Freddie,' sighed his mother, rubbing his hair dry, 'I'm sick of you being so naughty at bath-time; it really wears me out. You can clean your own teeth, I'm going downstairs to see if Daddy's in yet.'

Freddie sat on the bathroom floor sucking his thumb. He was surrounded by little pools of water and patches of foam, the result of his battle. He hadn't won round one, but he was determined to win round two. He picked up his toothbrush, ran it under the tap, took the top of the tube, spread it here and there as if he'd spat it out in the bottom of the basin, and then got into bed feeling rather pleased with himself. He didn't know why, but he didn't enjoy his comic that night; he couldn't smile once, not even at Korky the Cat, who was usually his favourite.

The next morning, after breakfast, his mother said, 'Go and clean your teeth, Freddie. I don't want to have to start the day with a quarrel, so you can do it by yourself.'

Freddie climbed the stairs with a sly grin. He

put his toothbrush under the tap, made a few splashing and spitting noises, spread a bit of toothpaste around the bottom of the basin and gazed triumphantly at himself in the mirror. He smiled gleefully, but quickly closed his mouth when he noticed that his teeth were pale yellow.

For pudding that day, Mother made a blackberry pie and for supper he finished with chocolate mousse. Freddie was quite good in the bath that night and said he would clean his own teeth. After splashing the toothbrush around for a while he grinned in the mirror and was surprised to see his teeth were brownish-grey with blackberry

seeds stuck between the spaces. He didn't sleep well at all.

The next morning after the same performance had gone on, Freddie bared his teeth in the mirror and found to his dismay that his teeth were pale green, and dotted with blackberry seeds. Still, it was better than the boring business of teeth-cleaning, and he was careful not to smile at anyone that day and only spoke with his hand over his mouth, much to everyone's amazement.

That night he spent ages making teeth-cleaning noises, spitting and sploshing about. He was afraid to look at his teeth which was hardly surprising for now they were quite black and tasted foul – and little did he know, but the blackberry seeds had started to take root.

The next few days were misery; little shoots began to grow around his gums, and tendrils with small leaves kept popping out of his mouth. He had to keep pushing them back in again in case anyone noticed. He was afraid to speak, of course, and just answered his parents with a 'Mmmmm' or a nod. His mother didn't mention his teeth, but he couldn't help feeling he wished she would.

After four weeks of not cleaning his teeth, Freddie was a dreadful sight. His mouth was a tangle of weeds and he was so thin through not eating, and so lonely through not speaking, that his heart was breaking.

His mother, greatly distressed, called the doctor.

His examination was brief. 'This child has not been cleaning his teeth!' he said, shaking his thermometer gravely and trying to part the branches to insert it in his mouth. 'There's nothing I can do for him I'm afraid. He'll have to go to the dentist!'

Freddie's mother was horrified. 'Why, Freddie,' she exclaimed, 'you are a silly boy. You think you have been cheating me but really you've been cheating yourself, and look what it's led to. I've never seen such a ghastly sight in my life. Put on your coat. We're off to the dentist at once.'

The dentist was a jolly chap. 'This is the worst case of non-teeth-cleaning I've ever come up against, my boy,' he said, and set to work with his probes and files and tweezers, disentangling the jungle in Freddie's mouth.

Freddie was half an hour in the dentist's chair and his teeth were given a final polish with a tickly brush whizzing round on the end of the drill. Then the dentist handed him a mirror and said, 'Now smile, Freddie – that's how your teeth should look.'

They were rows of gleaming white pearls set in firm pink gums – a lovely sight. Nobody ever had to tell Freddie to clean his teeth again.

Acknowledgements

The compiler and publishers would like to thank the following for the use of copyright material in this collection:

Curtis Brown Ltd for 'Boffy and the Teacher Eater' by Margaret Stuart Barry from *More Stories for Seven-year Olds* and 'Isabelle the Itch' by Constance C. Green from *Isabelle the Itch*.

Dutton Children's Books, a division of Penguin Books USA Inc for 'Cheese, Peas and Chocolate Pudding' by Betty van Witsen from *Believe and Make Believe* edited by Lucy Sprague Mitchell and Irma Simonton Black. Copyright © 1956 by the Bank Street College of Education, renewed 1984 by the Bank Street College of Education.

Hamish Hamilton Ltd for 'Trouble with the Fiend' by Sheila Lavelle from *Trouble with the Fiend*.

Hatton and Baker Ltd for 'Freddie, the Toothbrush Cheat' by Wendy Craig from *Happy Endings*, published by Hutchinson.

William Heinemann Ltd for 'Friends and Brothers' by Dick King-Smith from *Friends and Brothers* and 'The Tidying up of Thomas' by Charlotte Hough from *Charlotte Hough's Holiday Book*.

Hodder and Stoughton Ltd for 'The Not-very-nice Prince' by Pamela Oldfield from *Helter Skelter*.

Methuen Children's Books for 'The Arguing Boy' by Leila Berg from *Tales for Telling*.

Penguin Books for 'The Boy who made Faces' by Eileen Colwell from *Bad Boys* compiled by Eileen Colwell (Longman Young Books, 1972), © Eileen Colwell 1972.

Even
Naughtier
Stories

Contents

Ultra-Violet Catastrophe!

Margaret Mahy

Sally's mother stood underneath a big tree looking up into its branches.

'Sally!' she called. 'Are you there, Sally?'

'She isn't here,' Sally called back. 'Something has eaten her. It's dangerous up here.'

'Sally, come down at once!' her mother called again.

Sally shut her eyes and answered, 'I'm not Sally. I'm Horrible Stumper the tree pirate.'

But it was no use. Horrible Stumper the tree pirate had to come down out of the leaves and the smell of spring and turn into Sally once more.

Sally was washed around the face and scrubbed around the knees. She had to take off her blue jeans and put on her best dress and her long white socks. Her hair was brushed until it shone and her ears went all red and hot. She was being taken to visit a cousin of her mother's called Aunt Anne Pringle.

1

Aunt Anne lived in the country, but not on a farm. Her house was called *Sunny Nook*, and it was full of things Sally was not allowed to touch.

'She doesn't like me even to *breathe*,' Sally said crossly. 'She fusses and fusses all the time and there's no one to play with.'

'You'll have to manage somehow,' replied her mother. 'Surely you can sit still for a couple of hours. I know Anne is fussy, and I know there are no children to play with, but you can't expect everything to suit you all the time. . . . Sometimes you have to suit other people. Oh dear, your knees still look dirty.'

'It's the scratches,' Sally explained. 'Knees are the worst part for getting scratched. I could paint faces on my knees and then the scratches wouldn't show.'

'Come on!' said Sally's mother in rather a sharp voice. 'Hurry up, or we'll be late.'

They caught the bus in time.

Sally had hoped that they would miss it.

Aunt Anne met them at the door of *Sunny Nook*. Sally could tell at once that she had not improved. She was tiny, and terribly clean and neat. She looked more like a freshly dusted china ornament than any real person. She smiled at Sally, and then talked over her head to her mother.

'I have Father staying with me for a month,' she said. 'It's rather awkward. Old men can be so

2

difficult, and he's very set in his ways, you know. The things he says! Sometimes I don't understand just what he's getting at, he uses such funny, long words.'

Sally's mother made an I'm-sorry-to-hear-that clicking sound with her tongue.

They went into Aunt Anne's tiny sitting-room. There on the flowery couch was a very clean, scrubbed-and-scoured, washed-up and brushed-down, little old man.

Sally thought Aunt Anne must have rinsed him out, and then starched and ironed him, and *then* polished him with a soft cloth.

'This is Sally, Father,' said Aunt Anne. 'Do you remember hearing about Sally? I told you we had a dear little girl coming to visit us.'

Sally's mother thought she saw a Horrible Stumper-look coming on Sally's face again. She began to talk quickly. 'Sally, this is Great-Uncle Magnus Pringle.'

Great-Uncle Magnus looked at Sally from under his wrinkly eyelids. He said something very mysterious.

'Ultra-Violet Catastrophe to you, young lady.' His voice was loud for such a clean old man – loud but not crackly. It was rather like guns at sea.

'Oh, don't start talking rubbish!' said Aunt Anne fretfully. 'Look, why don't you two take each other for a walk down to the corner, while we girls have a little chat by ourselves?'

Mother and Aunt Anne took Sally and Great-Uncle Magnus out of the house and pointed them down the road towards the corner.

'Be good and keep clean,' said Aunt Anne.

'Do look after each other,' called Sally's mother.

Sally and Great-Uncle Magnus walked along the country road in the country sunshine smelling the country smells of wet grass and cows.

They came to a thick dark hedge speckled with little white flowers.

Suddenly Great-Uncle Magnus stopped.

'Do you like to go through hedges?' he asked. '*I* do, and it's years since I've been through a good hedge.'

Sally stared at Great-Uncle Magnus, amazed at such thoughts in a great-uncle.

'I see a hole in this hedge,' went on Great-Uncle Magnus, 'and I'm going through it. . . . It would be a help to have you give me a hand up on the other side.'

'Shall I go first, then?' asked Sally. 'In case of danger?'

'That would be kind of you,' said Great-Uncle Magnus. 'I have this creaky knee, you see. It's a good knee, mind you. I've had it for years, but it *is* creaky.'

Sally scrambled through the hole in the hedge,

smelling its special hedge smell as she went. The hedge tried to hold on to her, as hedges do, but she got through safely. After her came Great-Uncle Magnus, breathing hard.

'Ah,' he said, as Sally helped him up, 'that was good. That was refreshing. Now what have we here?'

On the other side of the hedge the ground was swampy from yesterday's rain. In between the grass, muddy water was oozing. Grass tufts stuck out of puddles.

'It's a long time since I had a paddle,' said Great-Uncle Magnus thoughtfully.

'What are you doing?' cried Sally.

'Taking my shoes and socks off,' the great-uncle replied, and so he was.

Sally grinned. She sat down beside Great-Uncle Magnus and took off her shoes and her long, white socks, too. She had to help the great-uncle with a tightly tied shoe lace.

'She always ties my shoe laces as if she were choking my shoes to death,' said Great-Uncle Magnus.

Great-Uncle Magnus's pale feet sank greedily into the mud.

'Ah!' he sighed, 'there's something about mud, eh? Nothing else has quite that – that – *muddy* feel, has it?'

Sally was amazed again. She had not expected

5

to find a great-uncle who felt the same way about mud as she did.

'Ultra-Violet Catastrophe,' murmured the great-uncle to himself.

'What does that mean?' asked Sally boldly.

It's the *sound* I say it for, not the meaning,' Great-Uncle Magnus explained. 'Some people say, "Goodness gracious". That doesn't mean much – they say it for the sound. But *I* like to say something that sounds even better and more important.'

'Words usually mean some real thing,' said Sally carefully. 'For instance, I say "Horrible Stumper" and it means a tree pirate. Don't your good words mean anything?'

'They *do* mean something scientific,' admitted Great-Uncle Magnus. 'Something scientific and too hard to explain.' He started to paddle along through the grass and mud. He had a muddy patch on the back of his trousers where he had been sitting down.

'You see,' he said, as he went along, 'Annie's a good girl and she means well – but she treats me like one of her pot plants. She waters me and puts me in the sun and leaves me alone. Serve her right if I grew up the wall and put out flowers. After a while I begin to think I'm really turning into a pot plant, and then I sing to myself or use long words – "Ultra-Violet Catastrophe", I say, or, sometimes, "Seismological Singularity".'

'That's a *hard* one,' said Sally with great respect.

'Too hard for a pot plant!' Great-Uncle Magnus nodded. 'No mere pot plant would use words like that. *Then* I know I'm Magnus Pringle all the time.'

They came to a clear stream flowing over brown stones. On the bank above the stream a green tree spread wide, rough arms. Great-Uncle Magnus's sharp, old eyes looked up into the green arch above them.

'It's years since I climbed a tree, years and years,' said Great-Uncle Magnus. 'I'd climb this one if it wasn't for my fear of the tree pirates.'

'Oh, well – I'll just go up and check for you,' Sally offered eagerly. 'This is too good a tree to waste! And when I'm up, I can help you if your knee creaks or if it's too hard for you or anything.'

'There's nothing like a tree,' Great-Uncle Magnus remarked a few minutes later. 'It's good being up in a tree, up in the air and the leaves all around us. What do *you* think?'

'Ultra-Violet Catastrophe, *I* think,' answered Sally boldly.

'Just what I was thinking myself, Seismological Singularity!' said Great-Uncle Magnus. 'I think I'll sing a bit.'

He pointed his old nose to the sky and began to sing:

7

'Boiled beef and carrots,
Boiled beef and carrots.'

Sally felt very happy, sitting up there in the tree
listening to Great-Uncle Magnus.

Everything felt very alive . . . the tree with its
branches and bark and its spring leaves bright
against the blue sky. Sally pointed her nose at the
sky too, and felt the sun shine through the leaves
in hot, spring freckles on her face. The tree at
home and the tree here were like sunny rooms in
open, rustling houses. She looked down at the
stream below.

'Is it years and years since you made a dam
across a creek?' asked Sally.

'How did you guess?' Great-Uncle Magnus
said, wonderingly. 'It is certainly a long time ago.
I see some good stones down there, too.'

Somehow Sally and Great-Uncle Magnus were
not as tidy as they had been when they set out.

Making a dam did not improve things. When
you are making a dam it is easy to get damp and
muddy around the edges. They built a good dam
out of mossy green and brown stones. The
cunning water found a way over, or around, or
through – keeping them busy and silent for quite a
long time.

Then a sudden noise made Great-Uncle
Magnus look up. He cleared his throat carefully.

9

'Sally,' he said, 'don't be frightened, but just look behind you and tell me what you see.'

Sally looked under her arm at the bank behind her. A large brown-and-white cow was standing there, watching them. She had a very young brown-and-white calf beside her. She had very sharp horns. As Sally looked, she put her head down and pointed her horns at them. She gave a grumbling, angry, 'Moo!'

'Having a new calf can make a cow very cross,' Great-Uncle Magnus said, gathering up his socks and shoes. 'Not that I'm frightened of a mere cow but still. . . .'

'A cow with a calf isn't as mere as other cows, I don't think,' said Sally, gathering up her socks and shoes, too.

The cow started to come down the bank at them. Sally and Great-Uncle Magnus moved quickly. Sally was amazed at the speed a great-uncle can put on when there is an angry cow coming down the bank after him.

There was no hedge on the other side of the creek, but there was a barbed-wire fence. Socks and shoes were tossed across. Then Sally scrambled over it. As she did so, she heard the hem of her dress tear open. A moment later Great-Uncle Magnus's trousers tore, too.

Sally and Great-Uncle Magnus stood staring at each other while the cow mooed angrily at them from the other side of the fence. Then her calf called, and she hurried back to it. And, at that very moment, like other anxious, mooing cows, Sally's mother and Aunt Anne were calling down the road.

Great-Uncle Magnus shook his head slowly. 'I can't see myself,' he said, 'but I don't think your mother is going to be pleased with *your* appearance.'

'I don't think Aunt Anne will be pleased with yours, either,' Sally told him. They were both wet and muddy and stained and torn.

There was a most terrible fuss!

'How *could* you, Father, how *could* you!' Aunt Anne cried.

'It just happened, Annie,' said Great-Uncle Magnus in a humble voice.

Aunt Anne made them stand on newspapers on the path, while she brushed them and cleaned them as well as she could.

'It's just as well you're going home at the end of the week,' she said to Great-Uncle Magnus. 'I couldn't stand another adventure like this!'

'Very sorry, Annie,' said Great-Uncle Magnus in his humble voice. He looked at Sally's mother. 'Why don't you and Sally come to see me when I go home?' he asked. 'I've got a little place by the beach, and a little boat I paddle around in. I catch a few fish from the end of the wharf. You wouldn't be bored.'

'We'd love to come,' said Sally's mother. (She wasn't as upset as Aunt Anne, being used to mud and torn skirts.) 'I can see you two get on well together,' she added.

'We've got a lot in common,' Great-Uncle Magnus agreed.

They had been so long on their walk there was scarcely time for Sally to have a bite to eat before getting ready to go home.

Sally and Great-Uncle Magnus looked at each other and could not find proper words to say goodbye in, even if it were only for a short time.

'Hurry, Sally, we'll miss the bus,' called her mother.

Sally suddenly knew the exact words to say. 'Ultra-Violet Catastrophe!' she called back, as her mother waved to Aunt Anne with one hand and tugged her with the other.

Great-Uncle Magnus brightened up. 'Horrible Stumper to _you_, young lady,' he replied. 'I wouldn't wish to go on a country walk with a better tree pirate than you yourself.'

My Naughty Little Sister and the Workmen

Dorothy Edwards

When my sister was a naughty little girl, she was very, very inquisitive. She was always looking and peeping into things that didn't belong to her. She used to open other people's cupboards and boxes just to find out what was inside.

Aren't you glad you're not inquisitive like that?

Well now, one day a lot of workmen came to dig up all the roads near our house, and my little sister was very interested in them. They were very nice men, but some of them had rather loud shouty voices sometimes. There were shovelling men, and picking men, and men with jumping-about things that went, 'ah-ah-ah-ah-ah-ah-aha-aaa', and men who drank tea out of jam pots, and men who cooked sausages over fires, and there was an old, old man who sat up all night when the other men had gone home, and who had lots of coats and scarves to keep him warm.

There were lots of things for my little

14

inquisitive sister to see, there were heaps of earth, and red lanterns for the old, old man to light at night time, and long poley things to keep the people from falling down the holes in the road, and workmen's huts, and many other things.

When the workmen were in our road, my little sister used to watch them every day. She used to lean over the gate and stare and stare, but when they went off to the next road she didn't see so much of them.

Well now, I will tell you about the inquisitive thing my little sister did one day, shall I?

Yes. Well, Bad Harry was my little sister's best boy-friend. Now this Bad Harry came one day to ask my mother if my little sister could go round to his house to play with him, and as Bad Harry's house wasn't far away, and as there were no roads to cross, my mother said my little sister could go.

So my little sister put on her hat and her coat, and her scarf and her gloves, because it was a nasty cold day, and went off with her best boy-friend to play with him.

They hurried along like good children until they came to the workmen in the next road, and then they went slow as slow, because there were so many things to see. They looked at this, and at that, and when they got past the workmen they found a very curious thing.

15

By the road there was a tall hedge, and under the tall hedge there was a mackintoshy bundle.

Now this mackintoshy bundle hadn't anything to do with Bad Harry, and it hadn't anything to do with my naughty little sister, yet, do you know, they were so inquisitive they stopped and looked at it.

They had such a good look at it that they had to get right under the hedge to see, and when they got very near it they found it was an old mackintosh wrapped round something or other inside.

Weren't they naughty? They should have gone straight home to Bad Harry's mother's house, shouldn't they? But they didn't. They stayed and looked at the mackintoshy bundle.

And they opened it. They really did. It wasn't their bundle, but they opened it wide under the hedge, and do you know what was inside it? I know you aren't an inquisitive meddlesome child, but would you like to know?

Well, inside the bundle there were lots and lots of parcels and packages tied up in red handkerchiefs, and brown paper, and newspaper, and instead of putting them back again like nice children those little horrors started to open all those parcels, and inside those parcels there were lots of things to eat!

There were sandwiches, and cakes, and meat

and cold cooked fish, and eggs and goodness knows what-all.

Weren't those bad children surprised? They couldn't think how all those sandwiches and things could have got into that old mackintosh.

Then Bad Harry said, 'Shall we eat them?' You remember he was a greedy lad. But my little sister said, 'No, it's picked-up food.' My little sister knew that my mother had told her never, never to eat picked-up food. You see she was good about *that*.

Only she was very bad after that, because she said, 'I know, let's play with it.'

So they took all those sandwiches and cakes and meat-pies and cold cooked fish and eggs and they laid them out across the path and made them into pretty patterns on the ground. Then Bad Harry threw a sandwich at my little sister and she threw a meat-pie at him, and they began to have a lovely game.

And then do you know what happened? A big roary voice called out, 'What do you think you're doing with our dinners, you monkeys – you?' And there was a big workman coming towards them, looking so cross and angry that those two bad children screamed and screamed, and because the workman was so roary they turned and ran and ran down the road and the workman ran after them as cross as cross. Weren't they frightened?

When they got back to where the other workmen were digging, those children were more
frightened than ever, because the big workman
shouted to all the other workmen about what
these naughty children had done with their
dinners.

Yes, those poor workmen had put all their
dinners under the hedge in the old mackintosh to
keep them dry and safe until dinner-time. As well
as being frightened, Bad Harry and my naughty
little sister were very ashamed.

They were so ashamed that they did a most silly thing. When they heard the big workman telling the others about their dinners, those silly children ran and hid themselves in one of the pipes that the workmen were putting in the road.

My naughty little sister went first, and old Bad Harry went in after her. Because my naughty little sister was so frightened she wriggled in and in the pipe, and Bad Harry came wriggling in after her, because he was frightened too.

And then a dreadful thing happened to my naughty little sister. That Bad Harry *stuck in the pipe* and he couldn't get any further. He was quite a round fat boy, you see, and he stuck fast as fast in the pipe.

Then didn't those sillies howl and howl.

My little sister howled because she didn't want to go on and on down the roadmen's pipe on her own, and Bad Harry howled becuase he couldn't move at all.

It was all terrible of course, but the roary workman rescued them very quickly. He couldn't reach Bad Harry with his arm, but he got a good long hooky iron thing, and he hooked it in Bad Harry's belt, and he pulled and pulled, and presently he pulled Bad Harry out of the pipe. Wasn't it a good thing they had a hooky iron? And wasn't it a *very* good thing that bad Harry had a strong belt on his coat?

When Bad Harry was out, my little sister wriggled back and back, and came out too, and when she saw all the poor workmen who wouldn't have any dinner, she cried and cried, and told them what a sorry girl she was.

She told the workmen that she and Bad Harry hadn't known the mackintoshy bundle was their dinners, and Bad Harry said he was sorry too and they were really so truly ashamed that the big workman said, 'Well, never mind this time. It's pay-day today, so we can send the boy for fish and chips instead,' and he told my little sister not to cry any more.

So my little sister stopped crying, and she and Bad Harry said they would never, never meddle and be inquisitive again.

Jane's Mansion

Robin Klein

Jane liked pretending to be grander than she really was. One day she was walking home from school with a new girl named Kylie, and showing off as usual.

'We have five Siamese cats at our house. And a special iced lemonade tap.'

Kylie dawdled, hoping to be invited in.

'I'd ask you in,' said Jane, 'but my mother's overseas. She's a famous opera singer.'

'Wow!' said Kylie.

'She's singing in Paris. Our housekeeper, Mrs Grid, is looking after me. Our house has twenty-five rooms full of Persian carpets and antique furniture.'

Kylie looked at Jane's house, thinking that a house containing such splendours would somehow look different.

'Don't take any notice of the front view,' said Jane. 'My Dad built it like that to trick burglars.

Inside it's different. My father is a millionaire.'

She waved goodbye airily and went inside.

The house certainly was different inside!

The living room was carpeted with gorgeous rugs, and had a silver fountain labelled 'iced lemonade'. The cane furniture had been replaced by carved oak.

'*Mum*! Did we win the pools?' Jane yelled

excitedly! Her mother wasn't home, but a note had been left in the kitchen. It read:

FROM PARIS GOING TO MILAN TO SING TOSCA, AFTER THAT VIENNA. HOUSEKEEPER WILL LOOK AFTER YOU, LOVE, MUM.

Jane read the note and then phoned the factory where her Dad worked. A voice said, 'Sorry it's not possible to speak to Mr Lawson. He's overseas inspecting all his oil wells, diamond mines and banks.'

It was Jane's turn to say Wow!

She went into her room to change. Normally her room was a clutter of dropped clothes, unmade bed, and overdue library books. But now it was magnificent. It had a four poster-bed, and a TV set in the ceiling. Jane was so impressed that she hung up her school dress instead of letting it lie like a gingham puddle on the floor.

She ran all around the splendid house looking at everything. It was amazing that such a vast mansion could fit into an ordinary surburban block. The back yard was too stupendous to be called that. There was a sunken pool in a huge lawn. She couldn't even find the fences that separated her house from the neighbours'. 'Not that I'd want to, now I'm a millionaire's daughter,' she thought smugly.

At six a brass gong summoned her for dinner at a long table lit by a candelabrum. There was one place set. 'Don't put your elbows on the table, Miss Jane,' somebody strict said. It was Mrs Grid, the housekeeper, and she was just as impressive as the house.

Jane couldn't even resist showing off to her. 'I've got to go to the Youth Club,' she said when she had finished dinner. 'I won every single trophy. It's Presentation Night.'

'I'll have Norton bring the car round to the front door,' Mrs Grid said.

Jane waited by the front steps. A huge car drove up, and a uniformed man held the door open for her. Jane remembered telling Kylie that she had a chauffeur. She felt very important being driven to Youth Club like that. Everyone's parents had come for Presentation Night. She regretted that hers were overseas, specially when the club president announced, 'Trophy for the most advanced member – Jane Lawson.'

No sooner had Jane received the trophy and sat down than the president said, 'Cup awarded for callisthenics – Jane Lawson', and she had to go back. She won every single prize, but it wasn't nearly as nice as she thought it would be. After her tenth trip to the stage, the clapping sounded forced, and most of the parents were glaring at her.

When she got home she showed the trophies to Mrs Grid.

Mrs Grid only said, 'All that silver will take a lot of polishing. I've already got enough to do looking after this mansion.'

Next morning her father cabled that he was in Brazil buying coffee plantations. Jane rang Kylie to brag.

'My Dad bought me a pair of skates,' Kylie said excitedly. 'Want to come round and see?'

'Skates are nothing,' Jane scoffed. '*My* father bought *me* a *horse*.'

There was a loud neighing at the window, and she put the phone back and went to look. A large horse was trotting round in the garden. 'Put your horse back in the stable at once,' said Mrs Grid crossly.

'I don't want to,' said Jane, but Mrs Grid looked at her so sternly that she lied quickly, 'We have a groom to look after my horse.'

A bandy-legged man in jodphurs appeared and led the horse away. Jane was relieved, because she was really scared of horses.

She went for another walk around her mansion, finding a whole lot of things she'd lied into existence in past conversations with people. There was a trained circus poodle, a crystal bathtub with goldfish swimming round the sides, a real little theatre complete with spotlights, a gymnasium in the basement, and five Siamese cats. She had a marvellous time playing with all that, but she was starting to feel lonely. Mrs Grid was too busy and crotchety to be company. Jane rang Kylie again.

'Come round and I'll let you ride my horse,' she offered.

'You wouldn't come round to see my skates,' Kylie pointed out, offended.

'We've got a real theatre and a crystal bath with goldfish swimming round the sides. Come round to my house and play,' Jane begged.

'I'd better not,' said Kylie.

'Why not?'

'Your house sounds too grand. I'd be scared of breaking something valuable. I'd better just play with you at school.' She hung up.

Jane sat and looked at all her trophies, and tried to feel proud. But she knew very well she hadn't really won any of those glittering things. She'd only got them by lying.

She missed her parents dreadfully, and remembered that this weekend her Dad had intended to make her a tree house. But he was in Brazil instead. 'Where's my shell collection and my pig I made out of a lemon?' she asked Mrs Grid, starting to cry.

'I threw all that rubbish out,' said Mrs Grid. 'And there's no point moping. Your parents have to work very hard to keep you in the manner you prefer. You'll just have to wait till Christmas to see them. I daresay they'll be able to drop in for a few minutes then.'

'I'm getting my own speedboat for Christmas,' Jane boasted, lying automatically through her tears.

'That reminds me,' said Mrs Grid. 'This telegram arrived for you.'

STATE MODEL AND COLOUR PREFERENCE FOR SPEEDBOAT WILL HAVE DELIVERED DEC. 25 LOVE ABSENT PARENTS.

Jane bawled louder.

'Just as well you're going away to boarding school tomorrow,' Mrs Grid said. 'So I won't have to put up with that awful noise.'

Jane was shocked into silence. She remembered lying to the neighbours that she'd won a scholarship to boarding school. She didn't want to go. She wanted her own house to be the way it usually was, with her own nice comfortable parents in it.

'You could pack your things for boarding school now,' said Mrs Grid. 'I'll get Norton to drive you there early.'

Jane jumped up. She ran out of the house and down the street to Kylie's. When Kylie opened the door, Jane babbled feverishly, 'We don't have a swimming pool, lemonade tap, horse, groom, miniature theatre or five Siamese cats, and I'm not going to boarding school. My Dad's not a millionaire, he's a fitter and turner. And my mum can't sing for toffee. We haven't got any antiques or Persian carpets, and I didn't win any trophies at Youth Club. I'll never tell any more lies ever again! And we haven't got a housekeeper, or a chauffeur called Norton. Please come up to my house to play, Kylie.'

'All right,' said Kylie. 'I knew you were lying, anyhow.'

They went back to Jane's house, and Jane drew a big breath and opened the door. It opened into her usual living room with its old cane furniture, and she could hear her Mum in the kitchen, singing off-key. Jane ran and hugged her. 'Where's Dad?' she asked anxiously.

'Just gone up to get the timber for your tree house,' said her mother. 'You can take some scones into your room if you like.'

'My room hasn't got a four-poster bed or a TV set in the ceiling,' Jane said to Kylie before she opened the door.

'I didn't think it had,' said Kylie.

They ate their scones while they looked at Jane's shell collection and the pig she had made out of a lemon. The scones tasted much nicer than

Mrs Grid's cooking. 'We haven't got a gymnasium in the basement or a poodle or a speedboat either,' said Jane. 'I tell a lot of lies.'

Her mother came to collect her scone plate.

She was cross about something.

'Who stripped the enamel off the bath tub and put goldfish in the sides?' she demanded.

Having Fun

René Goscinny

This afternooon I ran into Alec on my way to school and he said, 'Suppose we play truant?' I told him that would be naughty and our teacher wouldn't be pleased, and Dad had told me you had to work if you wanted to get on in life and be an airman, and Mum would be sad and it was wicked to tell lies. Alec reminded me it was arithmetic this afternoon, so I said, 'OK', and we didn't go to school.

We ran off in the opposite direction instead. Alec started puffing and blowing and he couldn't keep up. I ought to mention that Alec is my fat friend who's always eating, so of course he isn't too good at running, and I happen to be really great at the forty metres sprint, which is the length of the school playground. 'Hurry up, Alec!' I said. 'I can't!' said Alec. And he did a lot more puffing and then stopped entirely. I told him it was no good staying here, or our Mums and Dads might see us and not let us have any pudding, and then there were the school inspectors who'd put us in prison and keep us on bread and water. When Alec heard this it made him much braver and he started running so fast that I could hardly keep up myself.

We stopped a long way off, just past the nice grocer's where Mum buys the strawberry jam I like. 'We'll be safe here,' said Alec, and he took some biscuits out of his pocket and started eating them, because, he told me, running after lunch like that had made him hungry.

'This is a good idea of yours, Alec!' I said. 'When I think of the others doing arithmetic at school I could laugh my head off!' 'Me too,' said Alec, so we laughed. When we'd finished laughing I asked Alec what we were going to do now. 'No idea,' said Alec. 'We could go to the pictures.' That was a great idea too, only we didn't have any money. When we turned out our pockets we found string, marbles, two elastic bands and some crumbs. The crumbs were in Alec's pocket and he ate them. 'Oh well,' I said, 'never mind, even if we can't go to the pictures the others would rather be here with us!' 'You bet!' said Alec. 'Anyway, I wasn't really all that keen to see The Sheriff's Revenge.' 'Nor me,' I said. 'I mean, it's only a Western.' And we walked past the cinema to look at the stills outside. There was a cartoon film on too.

'Suppose we went to the square gardens?' I said. 'We could make a ball out of old paper and have a game.' Alec said that wasn't a bad idea, only there was a man in charge of the square gardens and if he saw us he'd ask us why we weren't at school and he'd take us away and lock us in a dungeon and keep us on bread and water. Just thinking of it made Alec feel hungry, and he got a cheese sandwich out of his satchel. We went on walking down the road, and when Alec had finished his sandwich he said, 'Well, the others at school aren't having fun, are they?' 'No fear,' I said, 'and anyway it's too late to go now, we'd get punished.'

We looked in the shop windows. Alec told me what all the things in the pork butcher's window were, and then we went to make faces in the mirrors which are in the windows of the shop selling perfume and stuff, but we went away again because we saw the people inside the shop looking at us and they seemed rather surprised. We looked at the clocks in the jeweller's window and it was still awfully early. 'Great!' I said. 'Plenty of time to have fun before we go home.' We were tired with all this walking, so Alec suggested going to the bit of waste ground, there's no one around there and you can sit down. The waste ground is really good. We had fun throwing stones at the empty tin cans. Then we got tired of throwing stones so we sat down and Alec started on a ham sandwich out of his satchel. It was his last sandwich. 'They must be in the middle of doing sums at school,' said Alec. 'No, they aren't,' I said. 'It'll be break by now.' 'Huh! You don't think break is any fun, do you?' Alec asked me. 'You bet I don't!' I said, and then I started to cry. Let's face it, it wasn't all that much fun here all on our own, with nothing to do, and having to hide, and I was right to want to go to school even if it *was* arithmetic and if I hadn't gone and met Alec I'd be having break now and I'd be playing marbles and cops and robbers and I'm very good at marbles. 'Why are you howling like that?' asked Alec. I said, 'It's all your fault I can't play cops and robbers.' Alec lost his temper. 'I didn't *ask* you to come with me,' he said, 'and what's more if you'd said you wouldn't come I'd have gone to school too so it's all your fault.' 'Oh really?' I said to Alec in a sarcastic voice Dad uses to Mr Billings who lives next door and likes to annoy Dad. 'Yes, really,' said Alec, just the same way Mr Billings says it to Dad, and we had a fight, just like Dad and Mr Billings.

When we'd finished our fight it started raining, so we went away from the waste ground because there wasn't anywhere to shelter from the rain, and my Mum doesn't like me to stay out in the wet and I almost never disobey my Mum.

35

Alec and I went to stand by the jeweller's shop window with the clocks in it. It was raining hard and we were all alone there and it wasn't that much fun. We waited till it was time to go home.

When I got home Mum said I looked so pale and tired that I could stay away from school tomorrow if I liked, and I said no and Mum was very surprised.

The thing is, when Alec and I tell the others at school tomorrow what fun we had they'll be green with envy!

Pierre

*a cautionary tale in Five Chapters
and a Prologue*

Maurice Sendak

Prologue
There was once a boy
named Pierre
who would only say,
'I don't care!'
Read his story,
my friend,
for you'll find
at the end
that a suitable
moral lies there.

Chapter I
One day
his mother said
when Pierre
climbed out of bed,
'Good morning,
darling boy,
you are
my only joy.'
Pierre said,
'I don't care!'
'What would you
like to eat?'
'I don't care!'
'Some lovely
cream of wheat?'

'I don't care!'
'Don't sit backwards
on your chair!'

'I don't care!'
'Or pour syrup
on your hair.'

'I don't care!'
'You are acting
like a clown.'
'I don't care!'
'And we have
to go to town.'

'I don't care!'
'Don't you want
to come, my dear?'
'I don't care!'
'Would you rather
stay right here?'
'I don't care!'
So his mother
left him there.

Chapter 2
His father said,
'Get off your head
or I'll march you
up to bed!'
Pierre said,
'I don't care!'
'I would think
that you could see –'
'I don't care!'
'Your head is where
your feet should be!'
'I don't care!'

'If you keep standing
upside down –'
'I don't care!'
'we'll never ever
get to town.'
'I don't care!'
'If only you would
say I CARE.'
'I don't care!'
'I'd let you fold
the folding chair.'

So his parents left him
there.
They didn't take him
anywhere.

Chapter 3
Now, as the night
began to fall
a hungry lion
paid a call.
He looked Pierre
right in the eye

and asked him
if he'd like to die.

Pierre said,
'I don't care!'
'I can eat you,
don't you see?'
'I don't care!'
'And you will be
inside of me.'
'I don't care!'
'Then you'll never
have to bother –'
'I don't care!'
'With a mother
and a father.'
'I don't care!'
'Is that all
you have to say?'
'I don't care!'
'Then I'll eat you,
if I may.'
'I don't care!'

39

So the lion
ate Pierre.

Chapter 4
Arriving home
at six o'clock,
his parents had
a dreadful shock!
They found the lion
sick in bed
and cried,
'Pierre is surely dead!'
They pulled the lion
by the hair,
They hit him
with the folding chair.
His mother asked,
'Where is Pierre?'
The lion answered,
'I don't care!'
His father said,
'Pierre's in there!'

Chapter 5
They rushed the lion
into town.
The doctor shook him
up and down.
And when the lion

gave a roar –
Pierre fell out
upon the floor.
He rubbed his eyes
and scratched his head
and laughed
because he wasn't dead.
His mother cried
and held him tight.
His father asked,
'Are you alright?'
Pierre said,
'I am feeling fine,
please take me home,
it's half past nine.'
The lion said,

40

'If you would care
to climb on me,
I'll take you there.'
Then everyone
looked at Pierre
who shouted,
'Yes, indeed I care!!'

The lion took them
home to rest
and stayed on
as a week-end guest.

The moral of Pierre
is: CARE!

Mr Miacca

Amabel Williams

Tommy Grimes was sometimes a good boy, and sometimes a bad boy, and when he was a bad boy, he was a very bad boy.

His mother used to say to him:

'Tommy, Tommy, be a good boy, and don't go out of our street, or else Mr Miacca will get you.'

But still, on the days when he was a bad boy he would go out of the street. One day, sure enough, he had scarcely got round the corner, when Mr Miacca caught him and popped him into a bag, upside down, and took him off to his house.

When Mr Miacca got Tommy inside the house, he pulled him out of the bag and set him down, and felt his arms and legs.

'You're rather tough,' says he, 'but you're all I've got for supper, and you'll not taste bad boiled. But, body o'me, I've forgotten the herbs, and it's bitter you'll taste without herbs. Sally! Here, I say, Sally!' And he called Mrs Miacca.

So Mrs Miacca came out of another room and said, 'What d'ye want, my dear?'

'Oh, here's a fine little boy for supper,' said Mr Miacca, 'but I've forgotten the herbs. Mind him, will ye, while I go for them.'

'l right, my love,' says Mrs Miacca, and off

Grimes said to Mrs Miacca,
a always have little boys for

ar,' said Mrs Miacca, 'if little
gh, and come his way.'
u have anything else but boy-
ng?' asked Tommy.
dding,' says Mrs Miacca, 'but
likes of us gets pudding.'
ther is making a pudding this
Tommy Grimes, 'and I'm sure
me, if I asked her. Shall I run and

a thoughtful boy,' said Mrs
n't be long and be sure to be back
er.'

o on Tommy pelted, and right glad he was to get off! For many a long day he was as good as good could be, and never went round the corner out of the street.

But somehow, he couldn't always remember to be good. And one day he went round the corner

43

again and, as luck would have it, he hadn't scarcely got round it when Mr Miacca grabbed him up, popped him in his bag, and took him home.

When he got there, Mr Miacca dropped him out, and when he saw who it was he said, 'Ah, you're the youngster that served me and my missus such a shabby trick, leaving us without any supper! Well, you shan't do it again. I'll watch over you myself. Here, get under the sofa, and I'll sit on it and watch the pot boil for you.'

So poor Tommy Grimes had to creep under the sofa, and Mr Miacca sat on it and waited for the pot to boil. And they waited, and they waited, but still the pot didn't boil, till at last Mr Miacca got tired of waiting, and he said, 'Here, you under there, I'm not going to wait any longer. Put out your leg, and I'll stop you giving me the slip.'

So Tommy put out a leg, and Mr Miacca got out his chopper, and chopped it off, and popped it in the pot. Suddenly he calls out:

'Sally, my dear! Sally!' and nobody answered. So he went into the next room to look for Mrs Miacca, and while he was there, Tommy crept out from under the sofa and ran out of the door. For you see, it wasn't his own leg, but the leg of the sofa that he had put out.

So Tommy Grimes ran home and never went round the corner again until he was old enough to go alone.

The Naughtiest Story of All

Dorothy Edwards

This is such a very terrible story about my naughty little sister that I hardly know how to tell it to you. It is all about one Christmas-time when I was a little girl, and my naughty little sister was a very little girl.

Now, my naughty little sister was very pleased when Christmas began to draw near, because she liked all the excitement of the plum-puddings and the turkeys, and the crackers and the holly, and all the Christmassy-looking shops, but there was one very awful thing about her – she didn't like to think about Father Christmas at all – she said he was a *horrid old man*!

There – I knew you would be shocked at that. But she did. And she said she wouldn't put up her stockings for him.

My mother told my naughty little sister what a good old man Father Christmas was, and how he brought the toys along on Christmas Eve, but my naughty little sister said, 'I don't care. And I don't want that nasty old man coming to our house.'

Well now, that was bad enough, wasn't it? But the really dreadful thing happened later on.

This is the dreadful thing; one day, my schoolteacher said that a Father Christmas Man would be coming to the school to bring presents for all the children, and my teacher said that the Father Christmas Man would have toys for all our little brothers and sisters as well, if they cared to come along for them. She said that there would be a real Christmas tree with candles on it, and sweeties and cups of tea and biscuits for our mothers.

Wasn't that a nice thought? Well now, when I told my little sister about the Christmas tree, she said 'Oh, nice!'

And when I told her about the sweeties she said, 'Very, very nice!' But when I told her about the Father Christmas Man, she said, 'Don't want *him*, nasty old man.'

Still, my mother said, 'You can't go to the Christmas tree without seeing him, so if you don't want to see him all that much, you will have to stay at home.'

But my naughty little sister did want to go, very much, so she said, 'I will go, and when the horrid Father Christmas Man comes in, I will close my eyes.'

So, we all went to the Christmas tree together, my mother and I, and my naughty little sister.

When we got to the school, my naughty little sister was very pleased to see all the pretty paper-chains that we had made in school hung all round the classrooms, and when she saw all the little lanterns, and the holly and all the robin-redbreast drawings pinned on the blackboards she smiled and smiled. She was very smily at first.

All the mothers, and the little brothers and sisters who were too young for school sat down in chairs and desks, and all the big schoolchildren acted a play for them.

My little sister was very excited to see all the children dressed up as fairies and robins and elves and Bo-peeps and things, and she clapped her hands very hard, like the grown-ups did, to show that she was enjoying herself. And she still smiled.

Then, when some of the teachers came round with bags of sweets, tied up in pretty coloured paper, my little sister smiled even more, and she sang too when all the children sang. She sang, 'Away in a manger,' because she knew the words very well. When she didn't know the words of some of the singing, she 'la-la'd'.

After all the singing, the teachers put out the lights, and took away the big screen from a corner of the room, and there was the Christmas tree, all lit up with candles and shining with silvery stuff, and little shiny coloured balls. There were lots of toys on the tree, and all the children cheered and clapped.

Then the teachers put the lights on again, and blew out the candles, so that we could all go and look at the tree. My little sister went too. She looked at the tree, and she looked at the toys, and she saw a specially nice doll with a blue dress on, and she said, 'For me.'

My mother said, 'You must wait and see what you are given.'

Then the teachers called out, 'Back to your seats, everyone, we have a visitor coming.' So all the children went back to their seats, and sat still and waited and listened.

And, as we waited and listened, we heard a tinkle-tinkle bell noise, and then the schoolroom door opened, and in walked the Father Christmas Man. My naughty little sister had forgotten all about him, so she hadn't time to close her eyes before he walked in. However, when she saw him, my little sister stopped smiling and began to be stubborn.

The Father Christmas Man was very nice. He said he hoped we were having a good time, and we all said, 'Yes,' except my naughty little sister – she didn't say a thing.

Then he said, 'Now, one at a time, children; and I will give each one of you a toy.'

So, first of all each schoolchild went up for a toy, and my naughty little sister still didn't shut her eyes because she wanted to see who was going to have the specially nice doll in the blue dress. But none of the schoolchildren had it.

Then Father Christmas began to call the little brothers and sisters up for presents, and, as he didn't know their names, he just said, 'Come along, sonny,' if it were a boy, and 'come along, girlie,' if it were a girl. The Father Christmas Man let the little brothers and sisters choose their own toys off the tree.

When my naughty little sister saw this, she was so worried about the specially nice doll, that she thought she would just go up and get it. She said, 'I don't like the horrid old beardy man, but I do like that nice doll.'

So, my naughty little sister got up without being asked to, and she went right out to the front where the Father Christmas Man was standing, and she said, 'That doll, please,' and pointed to the doll she wanted.

The Father Christmas Man laughed and all the teachers laughed, and the other mothers and the schoolchildren, and all the little brothers and sisters. My mother did not laugh because she was so shocked to see my naughty little sister going out without being asked to.

The Father Christmas Man took the specially

nice doll off the tree, and handed it to my naughty little sister and he said, 'Well now, I hear you don't like me very much, but won't you just shake hands?' and my naughty little sister said, 'No.' But she took the doll all the same.

The Father Christmas Man put out his nice old hand for her to shake and be friends, and do you know what that naughty bad girl did? *She bit his hand*. She really and truly did. Can you think of anything more dreadful and terrible? She bit Father Christmas's good old hand, and then she turned and ran and ran out of the school with all the children staring after her, and her doll held very tight in her arms.

The Father Christmas Man was very nice, he said it wasn't a hard bite, only a frightened one, and he made all the children sing songs together.

When my naughty little sister was brought back by my mother, she said she was very sorry, and the Father Christmas Man said, 'That's all right, old lady,' and because he was so smily and nice to her, my funny little sister went right up to him and gave him a big 'sorry' kiss, which pleased him very much.

And she hung her stocking up after all, and that kind man remembered to fill it for her.

My little sister kept the specially nice doll until she was quite grown-up. She called it Rosy-Primrose, and although she was sometimes bad-

tempered with it, she really loved it very much
indeed.

The Christmas List

Margaret Rettich

Wolfgang and Susanne had written a number of things on their Christmas list, but one wish they underlined with thick, red-pencil lines: 'One night we'd like to stay up for as long as we want to.'

'Why not?' Mama and Papa said.

They celebrated Christmas Eve together, there were lots of presents, they had something good to eat, and when it was time, Papa and Mama said, 'We're tired now and we're going to bed. Good night.'

'That's right,' said Susanne, 'and don't forget to brush your teeth.'

'And don't read any more!' cried Wolfgang after them.

'We're much too tired for that,' said Mama and yawned.

When Wolfgang and Susanne were alone, they jumped into chairs and stretched out their legs. Then they ate lots of marzipan. Susanne decided she should cover her parents up and give them a good night kiss. She did so, and Mama and Papa let themselves enjoy it.

Then Wolfgang and Susanne went back to the living room and turned on the television. A choir sang endless Christmas carols, which was boring. On another channel there was news and the weather report.

'Why isn't there any children's programme?' asked Susanne.

'Just think,' said Wolfgang, 'all the children are in bed now.'

That pleased them very much.

They turned the television off again and went into the kitchen. In the refrigerator there were lots of good things, but they weren't hungry. They only drank some soda and went back to the living room. They sat down again.

'Terrific when you can stay up late,' said Wolfgang. Susanne nodded and yawned.

They read the books that they had been given as presents and then ate some more marzipan. Susanne got more soda from the kitchen, and since she had forgotton the glasses, they drank out of the bottle. Wolfgang spilled the soda on his sweater; it was cold and sticky. He pulled it off and tried Papa's new pyjamas on. Susanne thought he looked funny. Mama had received a slip, which she tried on.

'Hah, we're ghosts,' she whispered. She stuck her head through the door to her parents' bedroom, but Mama and Papa were sound asleep, so Wolfgang and Susanne withdrew.

They tried the television again. On every channel there was whistling and sparkling.

'It's broken,' said Susanne.

'Don't be silly. They've stopped for the night. All the grown-ups are in bed now. Who would they broadcast for?'

'For us, for instance!' answered Susanne. She sat very straight in her chair.

Wolfgang turned the set off again. It was very quiet.

Once the cupboard creaked.

The light was very bright.

'How long do you want to stay up, anyhow?' asked Susanne.

'Till morning,' said Wolfgang.

Their eyes burned so terribly that he turned the lamp off. He tripped over the soda bottle and fell against Susanne's chair. She pulled his hair, and it hurt. So he pinched her arm.

Susanne ran away from Wolfgang and hid in her bed. Wolfgang crept quickly under his covers so that Susanne couldn't find him.

When they woke up, it was dark outside again. Papa and Mama had been up for a long time. They had had breakfast, had gone for a walk, had

had visitors, watched some television, and just done nothing.

Christmas Day was over.

The Family Dog

Judy Blume

Nobody ever came right out and said that Fudge was the reason that my father lost the Juicy-O account. But I thought about it. My father said he was glad to be rid of Mr Yarby. Now he could spend more time on his other clients – like the Toddle-Bike company. My father was in charge of their new TV commercial.

I thought maybe he could use me in it since I know how to stand on my head. But he said he wasn't planning on having any head-standers in the commercial.

I learned to stand on my head in gym class. I'm pretty good at it too. I can stay up for as long as three minutes. I showed my mother, my father and Fudge how I can do it right in the living room. They were all impressed. Especially Fudge. He wanted to do it too. So I turned him upside down and tried to teach him. But he always tumbled over backwards.

Right after I learned to stand on my head Fudge stopped eating. He did it suddenly. One day he was fine and the next day nothing. 'No eat,' he told my mother.

She didn't pay too much attention to him until the third day. When he still refused to eat she got upset. 'You've got to eat, Fudgie,' she said. 'You want to grow up to be big and strong, don't you?'

'No grow!' Fudge said.

That night my mother told my father how worried she was about Fudge. So my father did tricks for him while my mother stood over his chair trying to get some food into his mouth. But nothing worked. Not even juggling oranges.

Finally my mother got the brilliant idea of me standing on my head while she fed Fudge. I wasn't very excited about standing on my head in the kitchen. The floor is awfully hard in there. But my mother begged me. She said, 'It's very important for Fudge to eat. Please help us, Peter.'

So I stood on my head. When Fudge saw me upside down he clapped his hands and laughed. When he laughs he opens his mouth. That's when my mother stuffed some baked potato into it.

But the next morning I put my foot down. 'No! I don't want to stand on my head in the kitchen. Or anywhere else!' I added. 'And if I don't hurry I'll be late for school.'

'Don't you care if your brother starves?'

'No!' I told her.

'Peter! What an awful thing to say.'

'Oh . . . he'll eat when he gets hungry. Why don't you just leave him alone!'

That afternoon when I came home from school I found my brother on the kitchen floor playing with boxes of cereals and raisins and dried apricots. My mother was begging him to eat.

'No, no, no!' Fudge shouted. He made a

terrible mess, dumping everything on the floor.

'Please stand on your head, Peter,' my mother said. 'It's the only way he'll eat.'

'No!' I told her. 'I'm not going to stand on my head any more.' I went into my room and slammed the door. I played with Dribble until suppertime. Nobody ever worries about me the way they worry about Fudge. If I decided not to eat they'd probably never even notice!

That night during dinner Fudge hid under the kitchen table. He said, 'I'm a doggie. Woof . . . woof . . . woof!'

It was hard to eat with him under the table pulling on my legs. I waited for my father to say something. But he didn't.

Finally my mother jumped up. 'I know,' she said, 'if Fudgie's a doggie he wants to eat on the floor! Right?'

If you ask me Fudge never even thought about that. But he liked the idea a lot. He barked and nodded his head. So my mother fixed his plate and put it under the table. Then she reached down and petted him as though he was a real dog.

My father said, 'Aren't we carrying this a little too far?'

My mother didn't answer.

Fudge ate two bites of his dinner.

My mother was satisfied.

After a week of having him eat under the table

we felt like we really did have a family dog. I
thought how great it would be if we could trade in
Fudge for a nice cocker spaniel. That would solve
all my problems. I'd walk with him and feed him
and play with him. He could even sleep on the
edge of my bed at night. But of course that was
wishful thinking. My brother is here to stay. And
there's nothing much I can do about it.

Grandma came over with a million ideas
about getting Fudge to eat. She tricked him by
making milk shakes in the blender. When Fudge

wasn't looking she threw in an egg. Then she told him if he drank it all up there would be a surprise in the bottom of the glass. The first time he believed her. He finished her milk shake. But all he saw was an empty glass. There wasn't any surprise! Fudge got so mad he threw the glass down. It smashed into little pieces. After that Grandma left.

The next day my mother dragged Fudge to Dr Cone's office. He told her to leave him alone. That Fudge would eat when he got hungry.

I reminded my mother that I'd told her the same thing – and for free! But I guess my mother didn't believe either one of us because she took Fudge to see three more doctors. None of them could find a thing wrong with my brother. One doctor even suggested that my mother cook Fudge his favourite foods.

So that night my mother broiled lamb chops just for Fudge. The rest of us ate stew. She served him the two little lamb chops on his plate under the table. Just the smell of them was enough to make my stomach growl. I thought it was mean of my mother to make them for Fudge and not for me.

Fudge looked at his lamb chops for a few minutes. Then he pushed his plate away. 'No!' he said. 'No chops!'

'Fudge . . . you'll starve!' cried my mother cried. 'You *must* eat!'

'No chops! Corn Flakes,' Fudge said. 'Want Corn Flakes!'

My mother ran to get the cereal for Fudge. 'You can eat the chops if you want them, Peter,' she told me.

I reached down and helped myself to the lamb chops. My mother handed Fudge his bowl of cereal. But he didn't eat it. He sat at my feet and looked up at me. He watched me eat his chops.

'*Eat your cereal*' my father said.

'NO! NO EAT CEREAL!' Fudge yelled.

My father was really mad. His face turned bright red. He said, 'Fudge, you will eat that cereal or you will wear it!'

This was turning out to be fun after all, I thought. And the lamb chops were really tasty. I dipped a bone in some ketchup and chewed away.

Fudge messed around with his cereal for a minute. Then he looked at my father and said, 'NO EAT, NO EAT . . . NO EAT!'

My father wiped his mouth with his napkin, pushed back his chair, and got up from the table. He picked up the bowl of cereal in one hand, and Fudge in the other. He carried them both into the bathroom. I went along, nibbling on a bone, to see what was going to happen.

My father stood Fudge in the bath and dumped the whole bowl of cereal right over his head. Fudge screamed. He sure can scream loud.

My father motioned me to go back to the kitchen. He joined us in a minute. We sat down and finished our dinner. Fudge kept on screaming. My mother wanted to go to him but my father told her to stay where she was. He'd had enough of Fudge's monkey business at meal times.

I think my mother really was relieved that my father had taken over. For once my brother got what he deserved. And I was glad!

The next day Fudge sat at the table again. In his little red high chair where he belongs. He ate everything my mother put in front of him. 'No more doggie,' he told us.

And for a long time after that his favourite expression was 'eat it or wear it!'

St Samantha and a Life of Crime

Joan O'Donovan

Brothers and sisters are supposed to love each other. Mum says God said we'd got to, and she nags us when we don't. And I try to love my brother, really I do; it's just that I'm not very good at it. George isn't good at it either, but he doesn't care and I care a lot.

Mum doesn't know I worry about this; but then, I haven't told Mum I want to be a saint. Only my best friend, Emma, who's eight like me, knows that I want to have a saint's career when I leave school. I think it'd be fantastic. I imagine myself doing miracles and blessing people while they curtsey and say, 'Thank you, St Samantha.' In my pretend dreams George doesn't want to curtsey, but I make him and he looks silly, and serve him right. The trouble is, though, they only pick you for a saint if you're really good, and that's hard.

We had our holiday early this year. It was

super going to the seaside while everyone else was at school, and I promised to bring Emma back a stick of rock. We stayed at a guest house called Bella Vista; and George, who's nearly thirteen, made friends with some boys who'd got a cricket bat, so he spent most of the time with them while I played with Mum and Dad. All went well till the last afternoon, and then Mum told George he'd got to mind me while she and Dad went shopping.

We were both furious. We'd have liked to go

shopping, too, but we were skint. I'd got fifty pence, but that was for Emma's rock which I planned to buy next day; and George just can't save. I'm afraid Dad's a bit like George, so it's always Mum who looks after the money and pays our bills.

It was a rotten afternoon. We went on the beach, but there was nothing to do and we weren't talking to each other, and at teatime George made me walk the longest possible way back. I sometimes wish I could get holy and still be allowed not to love George.

We were nearly at Bella Vista when George turned down a side street; and up some steps there was a funny old shop with a bulging front. A sign hung over the door: ANTIQUES.

'What's antikews?' I asked, forgetting I wasn't going to speak first.

'An-*teeks*,' George said, staring hard at something in the window.

I looked, and right at the front, with a ticket on it saying £5.00, I saw a tiny galleon; and, amazingly, *it was inside a bottle*! I gazed at it. I'd never seen anything I wanted so much in all my life.

'How do you get a ship into a bottle like that?' I asked.

'Shove it in flat then pull it up with a string, stupid!'

'Is it hard?'

'I could make dozens,' George said, 'only I wouldn't be bothered.'

So it wasn't the galleon he was looking at.

'George,' I said cautiously, 'if you could have something from here, what would you choose?' and he said without hesitation, 'That stamp, the one on its own in front of the beads.'

'Fancy paying a pound for a used stamp!' I marvelled.

'Don't be so ignorant; that stamp's worth thousands.'

'But it only cost a penny when it was new,' I said reasonably.

'Oh, shut up!' George looked broodingly at the window. 'I just wish I'd got five quid, that's all. I'd know what to do with five quid if I had it.'

'If I'd got five quid I'd buy the ship.'

'I could make you one for a pound,' George suggested, brightening.

'I've only got fifty pence,' I said, feeling for it in my pocket.

'Fancy wanting a dreary old ship anyway!'

'Fancy wanting a used stamp!'

We stared glumly in. An old man came to the door and looked at us.

'If I'd five quid,' George whispered, 'I'd beat that wrinkly down!'

'You mean you'd *hit* him?' I asked fearfully.

71

'Beat him down means get things cheap – I thought everyone knew that! And I bet he'd let me have everything in his crummy window for five quid.'

'I bet he wouldn't! Why, just the ship costs five pounds.'

'I tell you what,' George said impressively, 'if I beat him down I'll give you that ship for nothing.'

'You wouldn't dare beat him down!'

'I bet you fifty pence I would. *And* you can have the beads as well.'

'All right!' I said excitedly, deciding to take Emma a string of beads instead of rock; and, heart thumping, I gave George my fifty pence.

'Thanks,' George said.

'Well, go on!'

'Go on what?'

'Go on in and beat him down.'

'What, offer the man fifty pence *for all those things*? You're nuts!'

'But you said. . . .'

'I said I *betted* you fifty pence I'd beat him down *if* I had five quid. Well, I haven't got five quid, have I? I've only got fifty pence.'

'You haven't got fifty pence! That fifty pence's mine!' I yelled.

'No it isn't, you've just given it to me,' George said. So I hit him as hard as I could with my wet bikini.

My brother gave a blood-curdling scream.

'You've knocked my eye out!' he shrieked. 'I'm blind!'; and he hid his face in the hand that wasn't holding my money. The old man opened the door and said if we didn't clear off he'd call the police, so we ran away.

By now I was crying. I begged George not to tell Mum that it was I who'd knocked his eye out; and he said he wouldn't if I promised, strike me dead, not to tell her about the fifty pence. So I promised, and George took his hand away and I saw that he'd still got both his eyes.

'Ever been had?' he said, and bought fifty pence worth of sweets.

Next morning I woke up worrying about Emma's rock. I called in for Mum and Dad as usual, but Mum shouted from the shower telling me to go down; as I went, I noticed her money spread out over the table. I'd never seen so much money together before.

And then something awful sort of happened. I found myself hurrying downstairs on wobbly legs with a five-pound note stuffed in my sock.

Dad and George were waiting in the dining room. Dad asked how much pocket money we'd got left.

'None, worst luck!' George grumbled; so Dad smiled and produced two one pound coins. He offered one to me and I went scarlet with shame.

'No, Dad,' I said faintly, 'give it to *Save the Children*.'

'She's nuts!' George said. 'Can I have them both?'

I accepted a pound in the end, to buy Emma's rock. The five pounds was to make George keep his promise to beat the shopkeeper down and give me the ship.

Mum was very late coming for breakfast. She looked pink and upset; and when Dad asked what was wrong she snapped, 'Eat your egg, Arthur!' in that special voice she uses when she's got money worries.

And then I knew. I knew for certain. Mum had missed the five pounds. It had never occurred to me that she'd miss just one note.

'I've had enough,' I said, trying not to tremble.

'Me, too. Can we go?' George asked. 'I want to buy a stamp.'

'Be back by eleven, then!' mother said, glaring at Dad; and for once she forgot to tell George to mind me, and he'd gone before I'd even got down.

I almost reeled to the door. I could feel the money in my sock, and I was afraid Mum might notice the bulge and call me back. And all this misery was for nothing, as I realized now. Involve George? No fear! He'd take one look at the five pound note and tell Mum.

Then I saw a way out. I'd buy the rock *and* the

ship; and if I hid the rock in my suitcase so that nobody saw it, I could pretend I'd beaten the shopkeeper down and got the ship for a pound. Who was to know?

But just before I reached the side street where the shop was, I met George coming back. He showed me his stamp and asked where I was going.

'Mind your own business,' I told him.

'It is my business,' George said, 'I've got to look after you.' So he followed me, and when he wasn't saying how much profit he'd make on the stamp he was offering to help me spend my pound. I daren't go near the antiques shop, so I drifted up and down the front hoping he'd get fed up and go away. But I was the one who got fed up. By half past ten I'd had enough, so I went sulkily up to the kiosk and bought Emma's rock.

George was satisfied then. He'd got his stamp without getting the ship, and he knew I'd no money left.

'Mum didn't say I'd got to mind you *today*,' he said, and scarpered.

As soon as he'd gone I rushed back to the shop. George had seen me buy the rock, of course, so now it was the galleon I'd have to hide: and it dawned on me that a life of crime was more complicated than I'd thought.

Then suddenly I remembered what Mum had

said about a neighbour: 'Tainted money launched her on a life of crime, and now she's a jailbird.'

I stood stock-still on the pavement. A jailbird? Saint Samantha? It was too dreadful to think of! I fished the tainted money out of my sock and pushed it down the drain before it had got time to launch me.

I got back to find Mum and George waiting outside the Bella Vista with our luggage. I could see Mum had been crying.

'Mum thinks Dad's a thief!' George whispered.

'*Dad*? What's he stolen?' I whispered back, horrified.

'Five quid. Only Dad says he didn't; and now he's gone off in a temper and Mum says we'll miss our train.'

My head went light and buzzy, and before I could stop myself I was sick in the bushes. Mum looked at me hard.

'Did *you* take anything from my room, Samantha?' she asked.

'No I didn't! And I feel ill!' I wailed; and then Dad came back with a taxi and we caught the train after all. What's more, Dad managed to persuade Mum that she couldn't have counted the money properly in the first place, so there was peace again – peace, that is, for everyone except me.

I was too miserable to eat, and when we got home I went to bed without any lunch, tea or supper. But in the night, I woke up and couldn't go to sleep again thinking of food. I kept imagining mountains of buttered toast, and baked beans and fish and chips and jam sponge and apple pie; but I knew it'd be hours till breakfast, so when I couldn't bear any more I ate up all of Emma's rock.

I went back to school this morning. I was too embarrassed to speak to Emma, and now Emma won't speak to me so I don't think we'll go on being best friends. I'm still worried about stealing from Mum, too. I know I'll have to confess in the end; but it'd be a lot easier if I hadn't thrown away her five-pound note, which I don't think she'll understand. And that's another thing that's worrying me. I bet they won't pick me for a saint now I've handled tainted money.

George is fed up as well, and serve him right. He took his stamp to a dealer today; but the dealer said he'd been done because it was only worth ten pence, which, George says, means that the wrinkly man made ninety per cent profit.

Ninety per cent! Actually, I'm not quite sure what ninety per cent means; but it does sound an awful lot, so I've decided that if I'm not picked for saint I'm going to keep an antiques shop and get rich.

Acknowledgements

The compilers and publishers wish to thank the following for permission to use copyright material in this anthology:

J M Dent & Sons for 'Ultra-Violet Catastrophe' by Margaret Mahy from *Leaf Magic*.

Methuen for 'My Naughty Little Sister and the Workmen' and 'The Naughtiest Story of All' by Dorothy Edwards from *My Naughty Little Sister*.

Pixel Publishing (Australia) for 'Jane's Mansion' by Robin Klein from *Ratbags and Rascals*.

Blackie and Son Limited for 'Having Fun' by Rene Goscinny from *Nicholas and the Gang at School*.

Collins Publishers for 'Pierre' by Maurice Sendak.

Hodder & Stoughton Limited for 'Mr Miacca' by Amabel Williams from *The Enchanted World*.

William Morrow & Company for 'The Christmas List' by Margaret Rettich from *The Silver Touch and Other Family Christmas Stories*. Translated from the German by Elizabeth D. Crawford.

The Bodley Head for 'The Family Dog' by Judy Blume from *Tales of a Fourth Grade Nothing*.

Joan O'Donovan for 'St Samantha and a Life of Crime'.

Naughtiest Stories

Contents

The Boy Who Wasn't Bad Enough

Lance Salway

A long time ago, in a far country, there lived a boy called Claud who was so bad that people both far and near had heard of his naughtiness. His mother and father loved him dearly, and so did his brothers and sisters, but even they became angry at the tricks he played on them and the mischief that he caused by his bad behaviour.

Once, when his grandmother came to stay, Claud put a big, fat frog in her bed. Once, when the teacher wasn't looking, he changed the hands on the school clock so that the children were sent home two hours early. And once, when Claud was feeling especially bad, he cut his mother's washing line so that the clean clothes fell into the mud, and he poured a bottle of ink over the head of his eldest sister, and he locked his two young brothers into a cupboard and threw the key down a well. And, as if that wasn't bad enough, he climbed to the top of the tallest tree in the garden and tied his father's best shirt to the topmost branch so that it waved in the wind like a flag.

His parents and his brothers and sisters did all they could to stop Claud's mischief and to make him a better boy. They sent him to bed without any supper, but that didn't make any difference. They wouldn't let him go to the circus when it came to the town, but that didn't make any difference. They wouldn't let him go out to play with his friends, but that didn't make any difference either because Claud hadn't any friends. All the other boys and girls of the town were much too frightened to play with him and, in any case, their parents wouldn't let them. But Claud didn't mind. He liked to play tricks on people and he enjoyed being as bad as possible. And he laughed when his parents became cross or his brothers and sisters cried because he liked to see how angry they would get when he was naughty.

'What *are* we to do with you?' sighed his mother. 'We've tried everything we can think of to stop you being so naughty. And it hasn't made any difference at all.'

'But I enjoy being bad,' said Claud, and he pushed his youngest sister so hard that she fell on the floor with a thump.

Everybody in the town had heard of Claud's naughtiness, and it wasn't long before the news spread to the next town and the next until everyone had heard that Claud was the naughtiest boy in the land. The king and queen had heard of Claud's naughtiness. And even the Chief Witch, who was the oldest and the ugliest and the most wicked witch in the kingdom, had heard of him too.

One day, the Chief Witch came to visit Claud's parents. They were very frightened when they saw her but Claud was overjoyed, especially when she told him that if he promised to be very bad indeed she would allow him to ride on her broomstick.

'I believe your son is the naughtiest boy in the whole country,' she said to Claud's father.

'He is,' he replied, sadly.

'Good!' said the Witch. 'I would like him to join my school for bad children. We are always looking for clever children to train as witches and wizards. And the naughtier they are, the better.'

Claud was very pleased when he heard of the Witch's plan and he begged his parents to allow him to go to her school.

'At least we'd have some peace,' said his mother. 'Yes, you may as well go, if it will make you happy.'

3

'Oh, it will, it will!' shouted Claud, and he rushed upstairs to get ready for the journey. And so, a few days later, the Chief Witch called again on her broomstick to take Claud to her school. He said goodbye to his parents and his brothers and sisters and climbed on to the broomstick behind her. He couldn't wave to his family but he smiled happily at them as he flew away on the long journey to school, clutching the broomstick with one hand and holding his suitcase with the other.

Everybody was pleased to see him go. The people of the town were pleased. Claud's brothers and sisters were pleased.

'Now we can enjoy ourselves,' they said. 'Claud won't be here to play tricks on us now.'

Even his mother and father were pleased. 'He'll be happy with the Witch,' they said. 'He can be as bad as he likes now.'

But, as time passed, they found that they all missed Claud.

'It was much more fun when he was here,' complained his brothers and sisters. 'We never knew what would happen next.'

Claud's mother and father, too, began to wish that he had never gone away. Even though he was such a bad boy they loved him dearly and wished that they had never allowed the Chief Witch to take him to school. And the people of

the town wished that Claud would come back.

'There was never a dull moment when Claud was here,' they sighed. 'Now, nothing ever happens in our town.'

As the weeks passed, Claud's family missed him more and more.

'Perhaps he'll come back to visit us,' his mother said.

But the summer ended and autumn passed and then winter came but still there was no visit from Claud.

'He'll never come back,' said his father, sadly.

And then, on a cold night in the middle of winter, they heard a faint knock on the front door.

'I wonder who that can be,' said Claud's mother, as she went to open it. 'Why, it's Claud!' she cried. And it was. He stood shivering on the doorstep, looking very thin and miserable and cold.

'We're so glad you've come back,' said his father. 'Sit down and tell us what happened and why you've come back to us.'

'I wasn't bad enough,' Claud said, and burst into tears. And then, when he had been given something to eat and had warmed himself by the fire, he told his parents about the school and about the very wicked children who were there.

'They were even naughtier than I am,' he

said. 'They turned people into frogs. They turned *me* into a frog until the Witch told them to turn me back. They were much, much naughtier than me. And even though I tried very hard indeed I just couldn't be as bad as the others. And so the Witch said I was too good ever to become a wicked wizard and she sent me away.'

'Never mind,' said his parents. 'We're very pleased to see you. We've missed you.'

His brothers and sisters were overjoyed at Claud's return. They laughed when Claud filled their shoes with jam while they were asleep. And they laughed when Claud tied them all to a tree. They even laughed when he pushed them all into the goldfish pond.

'Good old Claud!' they shouted. 'We're glad you're back!'

His mother laughed when she found out he had put beetles into the tea caddy. And his father didn't seem to mind when Claud cut large holes in his newspaper.

'Claud's back and quite his old self again,' they said, and smiled at each other.

But soon Claud found that being naughty wasn't as much fun any more. 'Nobody seems to mind my tricks,' he complained, 'even the new ones I learned at the Witch's school. People laugh when I trip them up, or tie their shoelaces together, or put ants in their hair. Why can't they be as angry as they used to be?'

So, because being bad wasn't any fun any more, Claud decided to be good instead. Not *completely* good, of course. Every now and again he would throw mud at his brothers and once he even covered the cat with a mixture of shoe polish and marmalade. But people soon forgot that he was once the naughtiest boy in the whole country. And the Chief Witch was so disappointed in Claud that she didn't call again.

Playing With Cuthbert

René Goscinny

I wanted to go out and play with our gang, but Mum said no, nothing doing, she didn't care for the little boys I went around with, we were always up to something silly, and anyway I was invited to tea with Cuthbert, who was a nice little boy with such good manners, and it would be a very good thing if I tried to be more like him.

I wasn't mad keen to go to tea with Cuthbert, or try to be more like him. Cuthbert is top of the class and teacher's pet and a rotten sport but we can't thump him much because of his glasses. I'd rather have gone to the swimming pool with Alec and Geoffrey and Eddie and the rest, but there it was, Mum looked as if she wasn't standing for any nonsense, and anyway I always do what my mum says, especially when she looks as if she isn't standing for any nonsense.

Mum made me wash and comb my hair and told me to put on my blue sailor suit with the nice creases in the trousers, and my white silk shirt and spotted tie. I had to wear that lot for my cousin Angela's wedding, the time I was sick after the reception.

'And don't look like that!' said Mum. 'You'll have a very nice time playing with Cuthbert, I'm sure.'

Then we went out. I was scared stiff of meeting the gang. They'd have laughed like a drain to see me got up like that!

Cuthbert's mum opened the door. 'Oh, isn't he sweet!' she said, and she hugged me and then she called Cuthbert. 'Cuthbert! Come along. Here's your little friend Nicholas.' So Cuthbert came along, he was all dressed up too, with velvet trousers and white socks and funny shiny black sandals. We looked a pair of right Charlies, him and me.

Cuthbert didn't look all that pleased to see me either, he shook my hand and his hand was all limp. 'Well, I'll be off,' said Mum. 'I hope he'll behave, and I'll be back to pick him up at six.' And Cuthbert's mum said she was sure we'd play nicely and I'd be very good. Mum gave me a rather worried look and then she went away.

We had tea. That was OK, there was choc-

olate to drink and jam and cake and biscuits and we didn't put our elbows on the table. After tea Cuthbert's mum told us to go and have a nice game in Cuthbert's room.

Up in his room Cuthbert started by telling me I mustn't thump him because he wore glasses and if I did he'd start to shout and his mum would have me put in prison. I told him I'd just love to thump him, but I wasn't going to because I'd promised my mum to be good. Cuthbert seemed to like the sound of that, and he said right, we'd play. He got out heaps of books: geography books and science books and arithmetic books, and he said we could read and do some sums to pass the time. He told me he knew some brilliant problems about the water from taps running into a bath with the plug pulled out so the bath emptied at the same time as it was filling.

That didn't sound like a bad idea, and I asked Cuthbert if I could see his bath because it might be fun. Cuthbert looked at me, took off his glasses, wiped them, thought a minute and then told me to come with him.

There was a big bath in the bathroom and I said why didn't we fill it and sail boats on it? Cuthbert said he'd never thought of that, but it was quite a good idea. The bath didn't take long to fill right up to the top (we put the plug in, not like the problem). But then we were stuck because Cuthbert didn't have any boats to sail in it. He explained that he didn't have many toys at all, he mostly had books. But luckily I can make paper boats and we took some pages out of his arithmetic book. Of course we tried to be careful so that Cuthbert could stick the pages back in the book afterwards, because it's very naughty to harm a book, a tree or a poor dumb animal.

We had a really great time. Cuthbert swished his arm about in the water to make waves. It was a pity he didn't roll up his shirt-sleeves first, and he didn't take off the watch he got for coming first in the last history test we had and now it says twenty past four all the time. After a bit longer, I don't know just how much longer because of the watch not working, we'd had enough of playing boats. Anyway there was water all over the place and we didn't want to make too much mess because there were muddy puddles on the floor and Cuthbert's sandals weren't as shiny as they used to be.

We went back to Cuthbert's room and he showed me his globe, which is a big metal ball on a stand with seas and continents and things on it. Cuthbert explained that it was for learning geography and finding where the different countries were. I knew that already, there's a globe like that at school and our teacher showed us how it works. Cuthbert told me you could unscrew his globe, and then it was like a big ball. I think it was me that got the idea of playing ball with it, only that turned out not to be such a very good idea after all. We did have some fun throwing and catching the globe, but Cuthbert had taken off his glasses so as not to risk breaking them, and he doesn't see very well without his glasses, so he missed the globe and the part with Australia on it hit his mirror and the mirror got broken. Cuthbert put his glasses on again to see what had happened and he was very upset. We put the globe back on its stand and decided to be more careful in case our mums weren't too pleased.

So we looked for something else to do, and Cuthbert told me his dad had given him a chemistry set to help him with science. He showed me the chemistry set; it's brilliant. It's a big box full of tubes and funny round bottles and little flasks full of things all different colours, and a spirit burner too. Cuthbert told me you could do some very instructive experiments with this chemistry set.

He started pouring little bits of powder and liquid into the tubes and they changed colour and went red or blue and now and then there was a puff of white smoke. It was ever so instructive. I told Cuthbert we ought to try something even more instructive, and he agreed. We took the biggest bottle and tipped all the powders and liquids into it and then we got the spirit burner and heated up the bottle. It was OK to start with; the stuff began frothing up, and then there was some very black smoke. The trouble was the smoke didn't smell too good and it made everything very dirty. When the bottle burst we had to stop the experiment.

Cuthbert started howling that he couldn't see any more, but luckily it was only because the lenses of his glasses were all black, and while he wiped them I opened the window, because the

smoke was making us cough. And the froth was making funny noises on the carpet, like boiling water, and the walls were all black and we weren't terribly clean ourselves.

Then Cuthbert's mum came in. For a moment she didn't say anything at all, just opened her eyes and her mouth very wide, and then she started to shout, she took off Cuthbert's glasses and she slapped him, and then she led us off to the bathroom to get washed. When Cuthbert's mum saw the bathroom she wasn't too pleased about that either.

Cuthbert was hanging on to his glasses for dear life, so as not to get slapped again. Cuthbert's mum went off telling me she was going to ring my mother and ask her to come and fetch me immediately and she'd never seen anything like it in all her born days and it was absolutely incredible.

Mum did come to fetch me pretty soon, and I was pleased because I wasn't having so much fun at Cuthbert's house any more, not with his mum carrying on like that. Mum took me home, telling me all the way she supposed I was proud of myself and I wouldn't have any pudding this evening. I must say, that was fair enough, because we did do one or two daft things at Cuthbert's. And actually Mum was right, as usual: I *did* have a nice time playing with Cuthbert. I'd have liked to go and see him again, but it seems that Cuthbert's mum doesn't want him to be friends with me.

Honestly, mothers! I do wish they could make up their minds, you just don't know *who* to play with!

The Crooked Little Finger

Philippa Pearce

One morning Judy woke up with a funny feeling in her little finger. It didn't exactly hurt; but it was beginning to ache and it was beginning to itch. It felt wrong. She held it straight out, and it still felt wrong. She curved it in on itself, with all the other fingers, and it still felt wrong.

In the end, she got dressed and went down to breakfast, holding that little finger straight up in the air, quite separately.

She sat down to breakfast, and said to her mother and her father and to her big brother, David, and her young sister, Daisy: 'My little finger's gone wrong.'

David asked: 'What have you done to it?'

'Nothing,' said Judy. 'I just woke up this morning and it somehow felt wrong.'

Her mother said: 'I expect you'll wake up tomorrow morning and it'll somehow feel right.'

'What about today though?' asked Judy; but

17

her mother wasn't listening any more.

Her father said: 'You haven't broken a bone in your little finger, have you, Judy? Can you bend it? Can you crook it – like this – as though you were beckoning with it?'

'Yes,' said Judy; and then 'Ooooow!'

'Did it hurt, then?' said her mother, suddenly listening again, and anxious.

'No,' said Judy. 'It didn't hurt at all when I crooked it. But it felt *very* funny. It felt wrong. I didn't like it.'

David said: 'I'm tired of Judy's little finger'; and their mother said: 'Forget your little finger, Judy, and get on with your breakfast.'

So Judy stopped talking about her little finger, but she couldn't forget it. It felt so odd. She tried crooking it again, and discovered that it wanted to crook itself. That was what it had been aching to do and itching to do.

She crooked it while she poured milk on her cereal and then waited for David to finish with the sugar.

Suddenly –

'Hey!' David cried angrily. 'Don't *do* that, Judy!'

'What is it now?' exclaimed their mother, startled.

'She snatched the sugar from under my nose, just when I was helping myself.' He was still holding the sugar spoon in the air.

'I didn't!' said Judy.

'You did!' said David. 'How else did the sugar get from me to you like that?'

'I crooked my little finger at it,' said Judy.

David said: 'What rubbish!'; and their mother said: 'Pass the sugar back to David at once, Judy.'

Their father said nothing, but stared at Judy's little finger; and Daisy said: 'The sugar went quick through the air. I saw it.' But nobody paid any attention to Daisy, of course.

Judy began to say: 'My little finger – '

But her mother interrupted her: 'Judy, we don't want to hear any more at all about that little finger. There's nothing wrong with it.'

So Judy said no more at all about her little finger; but it went on feeling very wrong.

Her father was the first to go, off to work. He kissed his wife goodbye, and his baby daughter, Daisy. He said, 'Be a good boy!' to David, and he said, 'Be a good girl!' to Judy. Then he stopped and kissed Judy, which he didn't usually do in the morning rush, and he whispered in her ear: 'Watch out for that little finger of yours that wants to be crooked!'

Then he went off to work; and, a little later, Judy and David went off to school.

And Judy's little finger still felt wrong, aching

and itching in its strange way.

Judy sat in her usual place in the classroom, listening to Mrs Potter reading a story aloud. While she listened, Judy looked round the classroom, and caught sight of an india-rubber she had often seen before and wished was hers. The india-rubber was shaped and coloured just like a perfect little pink pig with a roving eye. It belonged to a boy called Simon, whom she didn't know very well. Even if they had known each other very well indeed, he probably wouldn't have wanted to give Judy his perfect pink pig india-rubber.

As it was, Judy just stared at the india-rubber and longed to have it. While she longed, her

little finger began to ache very much indeed and to itch very much indeed. It ached and itched to be allowed to crook itself, to beckon.

In the end Judy crooked her little finger.

Then there was a tiny sound like a puff of breath, and something came sailing through the air from Simon's table to Judy's table, and it landed with a little *flop!* just by Judy's hand. And Mrs Potter had stopped reading the story, and was crying: 'Whatever are you doing, Simon Smith, to be throwing india-rubbers about? We don't throw india-rubbers about in this classroom!'

'I didn't throw my india-rubber!' said Simon.

He was very much flustered.

'Then how does it happen to be here?' Mrs Potter had come over to Judy's table to pick up the india-rubber. She turned it over, and there was SIMON SMITH written in ink on the underside.

Simon said nothing; and, of course, Judy said nothing; and Mrs Potter said: 'We *never* throw india-rubbers about in this classroom, Simon. I shall put this india-rubber up on my desk, and there it stays until the dinner-break.'

But it didn't stay there – oh, no! Judy waited and waited until no one in the classroom – no one at all – was looking; and then she crooked her little finger, and the india-rubber came sailing through the air again – *flop!* on to her table, just beside her. This time Judy picked it up very quickly and quietly and put it into her pocket.

At the end of the morning, Simon went up to Mrs Potter's desk to get his india-rubber back again; and it wasn't there. He searched round about, and so did Mrs Potter, but they couldn't find the india-rubber. In the end, Mrs Potter was bothered and cross, and Simon was crying. They had no idea where the india-rubber could have got to.

But Judy knew exactly where it was.

Now Judy knew what her little finger could do – what it ached and itched to be allowed to do. But she didn't want anyone else to know what it could do. That would have spoilt everything. She would have had to return Simon's pink pig india-rubber and anything else her little finger crooked itself to get.

So she was very, very careful. At dinner time she managed to crook her little finger at a second helping of syrup pudding, when no one was looking; and she got it, and ate it. Later on, she crooked her little finger at the prettiest seashell on the nature table, and no one saw it come through the air to her; and she put it into her pocket with the pink pig india-rubber. Later still, she crooked her finger at another girl's hair-ribbon, that was hanging loose, and at a useful two-coloured pencil. By the end of the school day, the pocket with the pink pig india-rubber was crammed full of things which did not belong to Judy but which had come to her when she crooked her little finger.

And what did Judy feel like? Right in the middle of her – in her stomach – she felt a heaviness, because she had eaten too much syrup pudding.

In her head, at the very top of her head, there was a fizziness of airy excitement that made her feel almost giddy.

And somewhere between the top of her head and her stomach she felt uncomfortable. She

23

wanted to think about all the things hidden in her pocket, and to enjoy the thought; but, on the other hand, she didn't want to think about them at all. Especially she didn't want to think about Simon Smith crying and crying for his pink pig india-rubber. The wanting to think and the *not* wanting to think made her feel very uncomfortable indeed.

When school was over, Judy went home with her brother David, as usual. They were passing the sweet shop, not far from their home, when Judy said: 'I'd like some chocolate, or some toffees.'

'You haven't any money to buy chocolate or toffees,' said David. 'Nor have I. Come on, Judy.'

Judy said: 'Daisy once went in there, and the shopman gave her a toffee. She hadn't any money, and he *gave* her a toffee.'

'That's because she was so little – a baby, really,' said David. 'He wouldn't give you a toffee, if you hadn't money to buy it.'

'It's not fair,' said Judy. And her little finger felt as if it agreed with her: it ached and it itched, and it longed to crook itself. But Judy wouldn't let it – yet. She and David passed the sweet shop and went home to tea.

After tea, it grew dark outside. Indoors every-one was busy, except for Judy. Her mother was bathing Daisy and putting her to bed; her father was mending something; David was making an aeroplane out of numbered parts. Nobody was noticing Judy, so she slipped out of the house and went along the street to the sweet shop.

It was quite dark by now, except for the street-lamps. All the shops were shut; there was nobody about. Judy would have been frightened to be out alone, after dark, without anyone's knowing, but her little finger ached and her little finger itched, and she could think of nothing else.

She reached the sweet shop, and looked in through the window. There were pretty tins of toffee and chocolate boxes tied with bright ribbon on display in the window. She peered beyond them, to the back of the shop, where she could just see the bars of chocolate stacked like bricks and the rows of big jars of boiled sweets and the packets and cartons and tubes of sweets and toffees and chocolates and other delightful things that she could only guess at in the dimness of the inside of the shop.

And Judy crooked her little finger.

She held her little finger crooked, and she saw the bars of chocolate and the jars of boiled sweets and all the other things beginning to move from the back of the shop towards the front, towards the window. Soon the window was crowded close with sweets of all kinds pressing against the glass, as though they had come to stare at her and at her crooked little finger. Judy backed away from the shop window, to the other side of the street; but she still held her little finger crooked, and all the things in the sweet shop pressed up against the window, and pressed and crowded and pressed and pressed, harder and harder, against the glass of the shop window, until –

CRACK!

The window shattered, and everything in it came flying out towards Judy as she stood there with her little finger crooked.

She was so frightened that she turned and ran for home as fast as she could, and behind her she heard a hundred thousand things from the sweet shop come skittering and skidding and bumping and thumping along the pavement after her.

She ran and she ran and she reached her front gate and then her front door and she ran in through the front door and slammed it shut behind her, and heard all the things that had been chasing her come rattling and banging against the front door, and then fall to the ground.

Then she found that she had uncrooked her little finger.

Although she was safe now, Judy ran upstairs to her bedroom and flung herself upon her bed and cried. As she lay there, crying, she held her little finger out straight in front of her, and said to it: 'I hate you – I HATE you!'

From her bed, she began to hear shouts and cries and the sound of running feet in the street outside, and her father's voice, and then her mother's, as they went out to see what had happened. There were people talking and talking, their voices high and loud with excitement and amazement. Later, there was the sound of a police car coming, and more talk.

But, in the end, the noise and the excitement

died away, and at last everything was quiet. Then she heard footsteps on the stairs, and her bedroom door opened, and her father's voice said: 'Are you there, Judy?'

'Yes.'

He came in and sat down on her bed. He said that her mother was settling Daisy, so he had come to tell her what had been happening. He said there had been a smash-and-grab raid at the sweet shop. There must have been a whole gang of raiders, and they had got clean away: no one had seen them. But the gang had had to dump their loot in their hurry to escape. They had thrown it all – chocolates and toffees and sweets and everything – into the first convenient front garden. Judy's father said that the stuff had all been flung into their own front garden and against their own front door.

As she listened, Judy wept and wept. Her father did not ask her why she was crying; but at last he said: 'How is that little finger?'

Judy said: 'I hate it!'

'I daresay,' said her father. 'But does it ache and itch any more?'

Judy thought a moment. 'No,' she said, 'it doesn't.' She stopped crying.

'Judy,' said her father, 'if it ever starts aching and itching again, *don't crook it*.'

'I won't,' said Judy. 'I never will again. Never.

Ever.'

The next day Judy went early to school, even before David. When she got into the classroom, only Mrs Potter was there, at the teacher's desk.

Judy went straight to the teacher's desk and brought out from her pocket the pink pig india-rubber and the shell and the hair-ribbon and the two-colour pencil and all the other things. She put them on Mrs Potter's desk, and Mrs Potter looked at them, and said nothing.

Judy said: 'I'm sorry. I'm really and truly sorry. And my father says to tell you that I had a crooked little finger yesterday. But it won't crook itself again, ever. I shan't let it.'

'I've heard of crooked little fingers,' said Mrs Potter. 'In the circumstances, Judy, we'll say no more.'

And Judy's little finger never crooked itself again, ever.

Licked

Paul Jennings

Tomorrow when Dad calms down I'll own up. Tell him the truth. He might laugh. He might cry. He might strangle me. But I have to put him out of his misery.

I like my dad. He takes me fishing. He gives me arm wrestles in front of the fire on cold nights. He plays Scrabble instead of watching the news. He tries practical jokes on me. And he keeps his promises. Always.

But he has two faults. Bad faults. One is to do with flies. He can't stand them. If there's a fly in the room he has to kill it. He won't use fly spray because of the ozone layer so he chases them with a fly swat. He races around the house swiping and swatting like a mad thing. He won't stop until the fly is flat. Squashed. Squished – sometimes still squirming on the end of the fly swat.

He's a dead-eye shot. He hardly ever misses.

When his old fly swat was almost worn out I bought him a nice new yellow one for his birthday. It wasn't yellow for long. It soon had bits of fly smeared all over it.

It's funny the different colours that squashed flies have inside them. Mostly it is black or brown. But often there are streaks of runny red stuff and sometimes bits of blue. The wings flash like diamonds if you hold them up to the light. But mostly the wings fall off unless they are stuck to the swat with a bit of squashed innards.

Chasing flies is Dad's first fault. His second one is table manners. He is mad about manners.

And it is always my manners that are the matter.

'Andrew,' he says. 'Don't put your elbows on the table.'

'Don't talk with your mouth full.'

'Don't lick your fingers.'

'Don't dunk your biscuit in the coffee.'

This is the way he goes on every meal time. He has a thing about flies and a thing about manners.

Anyway, to get back to the story. One day Dad is peeling the potatoes for tea. I am looking for my fifty cents that rolled under the table about a week ago. Mum is cutting up the cabbage and talking to Dad. They do not know that

31

I am there. It is a very important meal because Dad's boss, Mr Spinks, is coming for tea. Dad never stops going on about my manners when someone comes for tea.

'You should stop picking on Andrew at tea time,' says Mum.

'I don't,' says Dad.

'Yes you do,' says Mum. 'It's always "don't do this, don't do that". You'll give the boy a complex.'

I have never heard of a complex before but I guess that it is something awful like pimples.

'Tonight,' says Mum, 'I want you to go for the whole meal without telling Andrew off once.'

'Easy,' says Dad.

'Try hard,' says Mum. 'Promise me that you won't get cross with him.'

Dad looks at her for a long time. 'OK,' he says. 'It's a deal. I won't say one thing about his manners. But you're not allowed to either. What's good for me is good for you.'

'Shake,' says Mum. They shake hands and laugh.

I find the fifty cents and sneak out. I take a walk down the street to spend it before tea. Dad has promised not to tell me off at tea time. I think about how I can make him crack. It should be easy. I will slurp my soup. He hates that. He will tell me off. He might even yell. I just know that he can't go for the whole meal without going crook. 'This is going to be fun,' I say to myself.

That night Mum sets the table with the new tablecloth. And the best knives and forks. And the plates that I am not allowed to touch. She puts out serviettes in little rings. All of this means that it is an important meal. We don't usually use serviettes.

Mr Spinks comes in his best suit. He wears gold glasses and he frowns a lot. I can tell that he doesn't like children. You can always tell when adults don't like kids. They smile at you with their lips but not with their eyes.

Anyway, we sit down to tea. I put my secret weapon on the floor under the table. I'm sure that I can make Dad crack without using it. But it is there if all else fails.

The first course is soup and bread rolls. I make loud slurping noises with the soup. No one says anything about it. I make the slurping noises longer and louder. They go on and on and on. It sounds like someone has pulled the plug out of the bath. Dad clears his throat but doesn't say anything.

I try something different. I dip my bread in the soup and make it soggy. Then I hold it high above my head and drop it down into my mouth. I catch it with a loud slopping noise. I try again with an even bigger bit. This time I miss my mouth and the bit of soupy bread hits me in the eye.

Nothing is said. Dad looks at me. Mum looks at me. Mr Spinks tries not to look at me. They are talking about how Dad might get a promotion at work. They are pretending that I am not revolting.

The next course is chicken. Dad will crack over the chicken. He'll say something. He hates me picking up the bones.

The chicken is served. 'I've got the chicken's bottom,' I say in a loud voice.

Dad glares at me but he doesn't answer. I pick up the chicken and start stuffing it into my mouth with my fingers. I grab a roast potato and break it in half. I dip my fingers into the margarine and put some on the potato. It runs all over the place.

I have never seen anyone look as mad as the way Dad looks at me. He glares. He stares. He clears his throat. But still he doesn't crack. What a man. Nothing can make him break his promise.

I snap a chicken bone in half and suck out the middle. It is hollow and I can see right through it. I suck and slurp and swallow. Dad is going red in the face. Little veins are standing out on his nose. But still he does not crack.

35

The last course is baked apple and custard. I will get him with that. Mr Spinks has stopped talking about Dad's promotion. He is discussing something about discipline. About setting limits. About insisting on standards. Something like that. I put the hollow bone into the custard and use it like a straw. I suck the custard up the hollow chicken bone.

Dad clears his throat. He is very red in the face. 'Andrew,' he says.

He is going to crack. I have won.

'Yes,' I say through a mouth full of custard.

'Nothing,' he mumbles.

Dad is terrific. He is under enormous pressure but still he keeps his cool. There is only one thing left to do. I take out my secret weapon.

I place the yellow fly swat on the table next to my knife.

Everyone looks at it lying there on the white tablecloth. They stare and stare and stare. But nothing is said.

I pick up the fly swat and start to lick it. I lick it like an ice cream. A bit of chewy, brown goo comes off on my tongue. I swallow it quickly. Then I crunch a bit of crispy, black stuff.

Mr Spinks rushes out to the kitchen. I can hear him being sick in the kitchen sink.

Dad stands up. It is too much for him. He

cracks. 'Aaaaaagh,' he screams. He charges at me with hands held out like claws.

I run for it. I run down to my room and lock the door. Dad yells and shouts. He kicks and screams. But I lie low.

Tomorrow, when he calms down, I'll own up. I'll tell him how I went down the street and bought a new fly swat for fifty cents. I'll tell him about the currants and little bits of liquorice that I smeared on the fly swat.

I mean, I wouldn't really eat dead flies. Not unless it was for something important anyway.

The Incredible Henry McHugh

Robert Fisher

I am the Incredible Henry McHugh
you should see the things that I can do!
(and I'm only two)
I can . . .
tie laces in knots
spit peas into pots
squirt all the cream
and scream and SCREAM!

I can . . .
leave toys on the stair
pour honey in hair
scatter fried rice
play football with mice
sit down on the cat
be sick in a hat
slam the door, flood the floor,
and shout 'more, MORE, MORE!'

I can telephone Timbuctoo –
and frequently do,
hurl mud pies and rocks
put jelly in socks
pull Dracula faces
and stick Mum's pins in unlikely places.

I can . . .
pinch, poke, tickle and stroke,
wriggle, giggle, rattle and prattle,
scrawl on the wall
spill paint down the hall
pick heads off the flowers
dribble for hours
and when things go wrong
I just sing my song.

I'M not to blame.
You know my name,
I am Henry McHugh
the INCREDIBLE!
(I'm only two).

Horrible Harry and the Deadly Fish Tank

Suzy Kline

We have a fish tank in Room 2B. Last time Harry and I counted there were twenty-five fish swimming around in it.

Twenty guppies.

Four neon fish.

And one black molly.

Then there was horrible Monday. This is how it happened. Sidney came to school mad. He was mad about Harry putting ice water down his back on Friday.

Even his hair looked angry. It stood on end. Sidney probably didn't bother combing it.

Miss Mackle looked at the Monitor Chart. 'Boys and girls, I will announce the week's new monitors. Sidney is Messenger, Doug is Paper Monitor, Ida is Ant Monitor, Mary is Plant Monitor, Song Lee is Sweeper, and. . . .' When she finally got to Harry she said, 'Harry is Fish Monitor.'

Harry immediately got up and went back to feed the fish. He turned on the light in the tank and took roll. Carefully he recorded the number in the Fish Roll Book.

Then he checked the temperature. It was in the green part of the thermometer – in the 70–80 degree range.

At lunch time, Harry fed the fish and then lined up behind me in the cafeteria. 'I have my favourite dessert, Doug,' he said. 'Two pieces of Mum's home-made fudge. I'm saving it for us on the way home from school.'

I drooled. I knew how good Harry's mother's fudge was. Chocolate, nutty, and mmmmm good.

After lunch when we were working on maths, Harry walked back to check the tank. Then he shouted, 'The black molly is floating on the water. She's DEAD!'

Everyone rushed back to the tank.

Miss Mackle opened the cover of the tank and took out the net. She scooped up the dead fish. Then she put her finger in the water. 'Why, the water is hot! Someone has been fooling with the temperature knob.'

Everyone looked at the thermometer. The mercury was way above the green zone. 'Who would do such a horrible thing?' Miss Mackle exclaimed.

Everyone looked at Harry.

I did too. Harry loves to do horrible things.

Miss Mackle waited for someone to speak.

Sidney spoke first. 'Harry is the fish monitor. He did it!'

'Do you know anything about this?' Miss Mackle asked Harry.

Harry shook his head.

Miss Mackle said we wouldn't be doing 'little theatre' that afternoon. She didn't feel like doing anything fun. She was too disappointed.

We just worked at our seats the rest of the afternoon.

It was a long day.

When Harry lined up at three o'clock, no one wanted to stand next to him.

Except me.

'Do you think I did it?' Harry asked as we walked home.

I didn't say anything. I wasn't sure.

'Doug,' Harry said. 'I wouldn't do anything *that* horrible. I plan on being a great scientist someday. With you, remember? I would never take the life of a single living thing. Not a beetle, or an ant, or a single blade of grass.'

I knew Harry never mowed the lawn. He told his mother he couldn't kill the grass.

We walked home without talking. We didn't even eat Harry's home-made fudge. We just didn't feel like it. The next morning, Harry made a poster and put it up by the fish tank. It was a picture of a tombstone and a graveyard. It said GOD BLESS R BLAK MOLLY.

Then in the top part was a bunch of fish with yellow wings and haloes flying around.

'What's that up there?' I asked.

'Fish heaven,' Harry replied.

Miss Mackle started the morning as usual with a conversation.

'Boys and girls, we need to talk about our fish. We are responsible for them. Somehow, we made an error.'

Sidney raised his hand. 'Harry is the fish monitor. He likes to do horrible things. Harry did it. He should stay after school.' Then he sat back in his chair and smiled.

I looked at Sidney. Then it dawned on me. Revenge. That's what Sidney wanted! He wanted to get even because Harry had put ice water down his back.

Harry raised his fist at Sidney. 'I wouldn't cook a fish like that.'

'Prove it!' Sidney replied.

'Harry,' Miss Mackle said, 'do you know anything about how the black molly died?'

Harry shook his head.

Everyone made a face. No one believed Harry but me.

'Did anyone see someone at the fish tank just before the lunch bell?' I asked.

Song Lee had her hand in the air for the *first* time.

'Yes, Song Lee,' Miss Mackle said. 'Did you see someone?'

Softly, Song Lee spoke, 'I see Sidney by the tank just before bell ring. He reach behind where knob is.'

Sidney sank down in his chair.

Miss Mackle glared at him.

Sidney looked at the teacher, then the class. His face turned red. 'I didn't mean to kill the fish. I just . . . just . . .'

'Just what?' Miss Mackle asked.

'. . . wanted to get . . .' Sidney's voice got softer and softer '. . . Harry in trouble.'

'We'll talk about it after school,' Miss Mackle said firmly.

Holiday with the Fiend

Sheila Lavelle

The trouble with Angela is that she very easily gets bored. She's not content to read a book or paint a picture or knit herself a scarf. She has to be plotting and scheming and causing trouble all the time, and the more people she can find to play her tricks on, the better she likes it.

A holiday boarding house is a great place for somebody like Angela, and she didn't waste a single chance. She put big black plastic spiders in all the bathrooms, and frightened the two lady schoolteachers out of their wits. She pinched all the room keys off the board in the hall and muddled the numbers up before hanging them back on the wrong hooks. And one night she even crept into the larder while everybody was asleep and changed all the labels round on the boxes and tins of food. So there was salt in the sugar container and flour in the rice jar and peaches in the tins labelled baked beans. It made

some of the meals a bit of a surprise, I can tell
you.

I kept on refusing to have anything to do with
her plans, and finally she stopped pestering me
to help her and just got on with it herself. I was
relieved not to be getting into trouble, but at the
same time I couldn't help feeling a bit glum that
I was missing all the excitement. It doesn't seem
fair that the wicked people in the world have all
the fun.

One morning Daniel and I came back from
our early walk and caught her sneaking out of
the dining room with one of her dad's muddy
hiking boots on the end of a long pole. I stared
at her in astonishment, and Daniel growled at

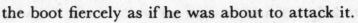

the boot fiercely as if he was about to attack it.

'Shurrup, you stupid dog,' hissed Angela. 'You'll wake everybody up.' And she shoved the boot into a carrier bag and hurried away upstairs.

I peered round the door into the dining room but I couldn't see what she had been up to. I didn't find out until we were all sitting at breakfast and Angela kept giggling so much she could hardly eat her scrambled eggs on toast.

'Look at the ceiling,' she whispered, when I begged her to tell me what was going on. I glanced upwards, and I almost choked.

Right across the white-painted ceiling from the doorway to the window were great big black muddy footprints. I looked fearfully at Mrs Down, but she was serenely serving coffee and fluttering her eyelashes at my dad.

'The rules say no muddy boots on the carpets,' murmured Angela slyly. 'They say nothing about the ceiling, do they?' She gave her tinkly little laugh. 'I bet you anything you like that nobody notices,' she said. 'People just don't look at ceilings.'

And do you know, she was right. I sat there fiddling nervously with my breakfast expecting that any minute somebody would give a shout. But not one person even glanced upwards, not during that breakfast or at any other meal for the rest of our holiday. As far as I know those muddy footprints are there to this day.

Snake in the Grass

Helen Cresswell

Robin could tell, right from the beginning, that
he was going to enjoy the picnic. To begin with,
Uncle Joe and Aunty Joy had brought him a
present, a bugle.

He took a long, testing blow. The note went
on and on and on – and on. He saw Aunty Joy
shudder and his cousin Nigel put his hands to
his ears. Nigel was twelve, and Robin hardly
even came up to his shoulder.

'We'll be off now,' Uncle Joe said, climbing
into his car. 'See you there.'

Robin got into the back seat of his father's
car.

'It's lovely at Miller's Beck,' his mother said.
'You'll love it, Robin.'

Robin did not reply. The picnic hamper was
on the back seat, too, and he was trying to squint
between the wickerwork to see what was in
there. In the end he gave up squinting and snif-

50

fed. Ham, was it? Tomatoes? Oranges, definitely, and was it – could it be – strawberries?

He sat back and began to practise the bugle. He kept playing the same three notes over and over again, and watched the back of his father's neck turning a dark red.

'D'ye *have* to play that thing now?' he growled at last. 'We shall all end up in a ditch!'

'I'm only trying to learn it, Dad,' said Robin. 'I've always wanted a bugle.'

An hour later, when they reached Miller's Beck, he had invented a tune that he really liked and had already played it about a hundred times. It was a kind of cross between 'Onward Christian Soldiers' and 'My Old Man's a Dustman'.

The minute the car stopped, Robin got out and ran down to the stream. He pulled off his shoes and socks and paddled in. The water was icy cold and clear as tap water, running over stones and gravel and small boulders.

Robin began to paddle downstream after a piece of floating bark he wanted for a boat, when:

'Ooooooooch!' he yelled. 'Owwwwwwch!'

A sharp pain ran through his foot. He balanced on one leg and lifted the hurt foot out of the water. He could see blood dripping from it.

'Oooooowh!' he yelled again. 'Help!'

He began to sway round and round on his good leg, like a spinning top winding down. He threw out his arms, yelled again and was down, flat on his bottom in the icy beck.

'Robin,' he heard his father scream. 'Robin.'

He sat where he was with the water above his waist and the hurt foot lifted above the water, still dripping blood. He couldn't even feel the foot any more. He just sat and stared at it as if it belonged to someone else.

His father was pulling off his shoes and socks and next minute was splashing in beside him and had lifted him clean up out of the water. Robin clutched him hard and water squelched between them. Robin's elbow moved sharply and he heard his father's yell.

'Hey, my glasses.'

Robin twisted his head and saw first that he was dripping blood all over his father's trousers, second that the bottoms of his father's trousers were in the water because he hadn't had time to roll them up, and third that lying at the bottom of the beck were his father's spectacles. Robin could see at a glance that they were broken – at least, one of the lenses was.

His father staggered blindly out of the water, smack into Uncle Joe, who was hopping on the bank.

'Here! Take him!' he gasped.

Then Robin was in Uncle Joe's arms, dripping blood and water all over *him*, and was carried back up the slope with his mother and Aunty Joy dancing and exclaiming around them.

It was half an hour before the picnic could really begin. By then, Robin was sitting on one of the folding chairs with his foot resting on a cushion on the other chair. This meant that both his parents were sitting on the grass. Robin's foot was bandaged with his father's handkerchief and the blood had soaked right through it and had made a great stain on the yellow cushion. Robin's shorts were hanging over the car bumper, where they were dripping on to Nigel's comic; Robin was wearing his swimming trunks and had his mother's new pink cardigan draped round his shoulders. There was blood on that, too.

Everyone's got a bit of blood, he noted with satisfaction.

Admittedly, his father and Uncle Joe had come off worst. His father sat half on the rug and half off with his trousers dripping. He had to keep squinting about him and twisting his head round to see through the one remaining lens of his glasses. Robin kept staring at him, thinking how queer he looked with one small squinting eye and one familiar large one behind the thick pebble lens. It made him look a different person – more a creature than a person, really, like something come up from under the sea.

'Are you comfy, dear?' asked his mother.

Robin nodded.

'Are you hungry?'

Robin nodded.

'Ravenous.'

'Pass Robin a sandwich, Nigel!' said Aunty Joy sharply. 'Sitting there stuffing yourself! And you'd better not have any more till we see how many Robin wants. Bless his heart! Does he look pale to you, Myra?'

The picnic got better and better every minute. Robin had at least three times his share of strawberries, and Aunty Joy made Nigel give Robin

his bag of crisps because she caught him sticking out his tongue at Robin. Nigel went off in a huff and found blood all over his comic and the minute he tried to turn the first page, it tore right across.

'That hanky's nearly soaked,' Robin said, watching Aunty Joy helping herself to the last of the strawberries. 'I've never seen so much blood. You should have seen it dripping into the water. It turned the whole stream a sort of horrible streaky red.'

Aunty Joy carried on spooning.

'If I'd been in the sea, I expect it'd have turned the whole *sea* red,' Robin went on. 'It was the thickest blood I ever saw. Sticky, thicky red blood – streams of it: Gallons. I bet it's killed all the fishes.'

Aunty Joy gulped and bravely spooned out the remaining juice.

'I won't bleed to death, will I?' he went on. 'Bleed and bleed and bleed till there isn't another drop of blood left in my whole body, and I'm dead. Just like an empty bag, I'd be.'

Aunty Joy turned pale and put down her spoon.

'Just an empty bag of skin,' repeated Robin thoughtfully. 'That's what I'll be.'

'Of course you won't, darling!' cried his mother.

'Well, this handkerchief certainly is bloody,' said Robin. 'There must've been a bucket of blood. A *bowlful* anyway!'

Aunty Joy pushed away her bowl of strawberries.

'I wonder what it could've been?' went on Robin. 'That cut me, I mean.'

'Glass!' his mother said. 'It must have been. It's disgraceful, leaving broken glass lying about like that. Someone might have been crippled for life.'

'Dad,' said Robin, after a pause. At first his father did not hear. He had stretched out at full length and was peering closely at his newspaper with his one pebble eye.

'Dad!' His father looked up. 'Dad, hadn't you better go and pick *your* glass up? From your specs, I mean? Somebody else might go and cut themselves.'

'The child's right!' his mother cried. 'Fancy the angel thinking of that! Off you go, George, and pick it up, straight away!'

Robin's father got up slowly. His trousers flapped wetly about his legs and his bloodstained shirt clung to him.

'And mind you pick up every little bit!' she called after him. 'Don't you want those strawberries, Joy?'

She shook her head.

'Could you manage them, Robin?'

Robin could. He did. When he had finished, he licked the bowl.

Once the tea things were cleared away, everyone settled down. Aunty Joy was knitting a complicated lacy jacket that meant she had to keep counting under her breath. His mother read, Uncle Joe decided to wash his car, and his father was searching for the sports pages of his newspaper that had blown away while he was down at the beck picking up his broken spectacles. Nigel had a new model yacht and took it down to the stream. Robin watched him go. All *he* had was a sodden comic and the bugle.

He played the bugle until the back of his father's neck was crimson again and Aunty Joy had twice lost count of her stitches and had to go right back to the beginning of the row again. For a change, he tried letting her get halfway across a row and then, without warning, gave a deafening blast. She jumped, the needles jerked, and half the stitches came off.

After the third time, even that didn't seem funny any more. Robin swung his legs down and tested the bad foot. Surprisingly, it hardly hurt at all. He stood right up and took a few steps. His mother looked up.

'Robin!' she squealed. 'Darling! What are you doing?'

'It's all right, Mum,' he said. 'It doesn't hurt.
It's stopped bleeding now. It looks worse than
it is, the handkerchief being all bloody.'

'I really think you should sit still,' she said.

Robin took no notice and went limping down
to the beck. Nigel was in midstream, turning his
yacht. It was a beauty.

'Swap you it for my bugle,' he said, after a
time.

'What?' Nigel turned to face him. 'You're
crazy. Crazy little kid!'

'I'll swap,' repeated Robin.

'Well, I *won't*.' Nigel turned his back again.

Robin stayed where he was. Lying by his feet
were Nigel's shoes, with the socks stuffed inside

them. Gently, using the big toe of his bandaged foot, he edged them off the bank and into the water. They lay there, the shoes filled and the socks began to balloon and sway. Fascinated, Robin watched. At last the socks, with a final graceful swirl, drifted free of the shoes and began to float downstream.

Robin watched them out of sight. After that, there seemed nothing he could do. What *could* you do, with your foot all bandaged up? The picnic was going all to pieces.

He felt a little sting on his good leg and looked down in time to see a gnat making off. He swatted hard at it, and with a sudden inspiration clapped a hand to his leg, fell to his knees and let out a bloodcurdling howl.

'Robin!' He heard his mother scream. 'Robin!'

They were thundering down the slope towards him now, all of them, even Uncle Joe, wash-leather in hand.

'Darling! What is it?'

'Snake!' gasped Robin, squeezing his leg tight with his fingers.

'Where?' cried Aunty Joy. He pointed upstream, towards the long grass. He noticed that her wool was wound round her waist and her knitting trailing behind her, both needles missing.

'Where did it *bite* you?' she cried.

Robin took his hands away from the leg. Where they had clutched it, the skin was red and in the middle of the crimson patch was the tiny prick made by the gnat.

'Ooooooh!' he heard his mother give an odd, sighing moan and looked up in time to see that she was falling. His father leapt forward and caught her just in time and they both fell to the ground together.

Biting the dust, thought Robin, watching them.

'Here!' cried Aunty Joy. 'We'll have to suck the poison out!'

She dropped to her knees beside him, her hair awry and face flushed. Next minute she had her mouth to Robin's leg and was sucking it, with fierce, noisy sucks. He tried to jerk his leg away but she had it in an iron grip. At last she stopped sucking and turning her head aside spat fiercely right into the stream. It was almost worth having her suck, to see her spit.

'Carry him up to the car!' she gasped, scrambling up. 'I must see to Myra!'

Uncle Joe picked him up for the second time that day and carried him away. Over his shoulder Robin could see the others bending over his mother, trying to lift her. Best of all, he could see Nigel beating round in the long grass with a stick while his boat, forgotten, sailed slowly off downstream.

Gone, Robin thought. Gone for ever.

Uncle Joe put him down in the driving seat of his own car.

'Be all right for a minute, old chap?' he asked.

Robin nodded.

'Have a mint.' He fished for one from his pocket. 'Back in a minute. Better go and see if I can find that brute of a snake. Don't want Nigel bitten.'

Then he was gone. Robin stared through the windscreen towards the excited huddle by the bank. It seemed to him that everyone was having a good time except himself. There he sat, quite alone, scratching absently at the gnat bite.

Idly he looked about the inside of the car. Usually he wasn't allowed in. It was Uncle Joe's pride and joy. The dashboard glittered with knobs and dials. He twiddled one or two of them, and got the radio working, then a green light on, then a red, then the windscreen wipers working. He pushed the gearstick and it slotted smoothly into place. To his left, between the bucket seats, was the handbrake. He knew how to release it – his father had shown him.

The brake was tightly on, and it was a struggle. He was red in the face and panting by the time he sat upright again. The car was rolling forward, very gently, down the grassy slope,

then gathering speed as it approached the beck.

By the time they saw him it was too late. The car lurched, then bounced off the bank and into the water. It stopped, right in midstream.

Robin looked out and saw himself surrounded by water.

The captain goes down with his ship! he thought.

He saw his mother sit up, stare, then fall straight back again. He saw the others, wet, bloodstained and horror-struck, advancing towards him.

With a sigh he let his hands fall from the wheel. It was the end of the picnic, he could see that. He wound down the window and put out a hand to wave. Instead, it met glass and warm flesh. He heard a splash and a tinkle. Level with the window, he saw his father's face. Now *both* his eyes were small and squinting. Small, squinting and murderous.

The picnic was definitely over.

Jelly Jake and Butter Bill

Leroy F Jackson

Jelly Jake and Butter Bill
One dark night when all was still
Pattered down the long, dark stair,
And no one saw the guilty pair;
Pushed aside the pantry door

And there found everything galore –
Honey, raisins, orange-peel,
Cold chicken aplenty for a meal,
Gingerbread enough to fill
Two such boys as Jake and Bill.

Well, they ate and ate and ate,
Gobbled at an awful rate
Till I'm sure they soon weighed more
Than double what they did before.
And then, it's awful, still it's true,
The floor gave way and they went through.

Filled so full they couldn't fight,
Slowly they sank out of sight.
Father, Mother, Cousin Ann,
Cook and nurse and furnace man
Fished in forty-dozen ways
After them, for twenty days;

But not a soul has chanced to get
A glimpse or glimmer of them yet.
And I'm afraid we never will —
Poor Jelly Jake and Butter Bill.

When I Lived Down Cuckoo Lane and Lost a Fox Fur, and a Lot More Besides

Jean Wills

'Next Saturday your aunts are coming to tea.'

I grinned at Mum, and she smiled at me.

The town aunts were good news. I could dress up in their clothes. Mum would have a good gossip. And we'd all enjoy a tremendous feast.

I asked if my best friend could come as well.

'As long as you're not noisy.'

'Noisy? *US?*'

I went and wrote a message and put it in the cricket post.

SATERDAY ARENTS DRESSING UP

It was our favourite game just then. We'd been mothers. Grandmothers. Queens and princesses. But never aunts. And the town aunts were really fancy dressers.

Next time I looked in the wall there was another message.

I looked up at the sky, and Pat and Mick ran out of the alley and captured me.

'So that's what they do with that wall,' Mick said.

The cricket post was a secret no longer.

Pat stopped whistling through his gap. ' "Cuming Sat God"?'

' "Cuming" is coming. "Sat" could be Saturday. And "God" is good,' said Mick. 'Amen.'

They both turned to me.

'What is happening on Saturday?'

I wouldn't tell them anything. My best friend and I were going to have the town aunts all to ourselves.

On Saturday afternoon we hid behind the wall to wait. We waited and waited.

'Suppose they don't come?' my best friend said.

'They're always late. They have to dress up, go to the shops, and catch the train. And the Number 5 bus. They'll come.'

Later on two people turned the corner, one short, one tall.

'It's them!'

'At last.' We started out, but my best friend stopped. 'You didn't say there'd be dogs.'

'What dogs?'

'The ones they're carrying.'

'They're furs. I told you. The town aunts are fancy dressers.'

'And eaters, you said.'

'And eaters too.' I pointed to the parcels.

We started to run.

The town aunts opened their arms out wide. They kissed us, called us 'dear' and 'darling', and gave us their parcels to carry.

We made so much noise walking down Cuckoo Lane that people looked out of their windows to watch. Mrs Thresher came out and leaned on her gate. The town aunts laughed, and swept into our house.

Leaving the parcels on the kitchen table we followed them upstairs.

Mum and Dad's bed was soon covered with coats. Hats. Gloves. Furs. The town aunts kicked off their high-heeled shoes. They patted their hair, and powdered their noses. The room was full of a lovely scent.

Then down we all went to open the parcels.

There were chocolate fingers. Coconut cream. Brandy snaps. An iced cake and walnut whips.

Mum made tea in her best silver pot. The best china stood ready on the best silver tray. There were cucumber sandwiches, sausage rolls, and a Dundee cake, as well as everything else.

We packed our share of the feast in the cake

box. When Mum and the aunts were safely shut up we crept back upstairs to the bedroom.

'What shall we do first?' my best friend said. 'Eat or dress up?'

'Dress up.'

My best friend wasn't sure.

'Then we can have a whopping big feast afterwards. And eat the whole lot in one go.'

I put on my tall aunt's mauve silk coat. Her black straw hat. And the high-heeled shoes.

'You do look funny,' my best friend said. 'Miss Baloni gone barmy.'

I didn't want to look like Miss Baloni, but my glamorous, exciting town aunt.

My best friend disappeared inside my short aunt's coat. She pulled on a hat like a chimney pot.

'*You* look like Green Hill.'

My best friend snatched up a chocolate finger.

'Not yet!'

'Why not?'

And that's when it all went wrong.

As I tottered forward to grab the cake box a cucumber sandwich flew out. My best friend trod on it and fell over. Clutching at the bed she pulled off a fox fur.

'Eurgh! I don't like it. Take it away!'

Instead I wriggled the fox fur towards her.

She climbed on to the dressing table. I threw

the fur, and she threw it back. It hit the window, and flopped on the ledge.

Outside somebody whistled.

'Did you see that?'

'It's not a cat.'

'Nor a dog.'

'Nor a rabbit.'

'It's a fox!'

My best friend climbed down. We crawled beneath the window. I reached up and wriggled the fox. And giggled. And wriggled. And the more I did the more I couldn't stop. And my best friend couldn't either. Until. . . .

The fur fell out of the window.

We got tangled up in the town aunts' coats. By the time we looked out Pat and Mick were in the alley, and the fox fur with them.

Downstairs a door opened. Shrieks of laughter blew up the stairs. Then Mum called.

'Are you two still up there?'

'Yes.'

'You're not to touch your aunts' things with your sticky fingers.'

If only that was all we had done!

'Go out into the garden.'

We laid the clothes back on the bed. Took the cake box, and ran downstairs.

Pat and Mick were in the alley, stroking the fox.

'Poor thing,' said Mick fiercely. 'How would you like it? Glass beads for eyes. Your insides out, and lined with silk.'

'It's not my fault,' I said.

'We'll bury it. That's what we'll do. Deep in the jungle, where nobody will ever find it.' Pat began whistling.

'You can't!' I said.

They walked away.

'I must have it back. I must, I must. I'll give you . . .'

'What?'

They stood at the top of the alley and waited.

I held out the box. '. . . some of this.'

They took the whole lot, and ran off with it.

After we'd put the fox fur back we went to see how far Mum and the town aunts had got with their tea. All that talking and laughing. . . . There couldn't have been much time for eating.

But. . . .

My best friend stared, and so did I. The best china plates were covered in crumbs, nothing else!

As we walked to the bus stop with the town aunts Mrs Thresher leaned on her gate to watch. Windows opened. The fox furs bounced on the town aunts' chests.

'Did you have a lovely feed, my darlings?'

We couldn't speak, just nodded instead. And

tried not to think about sausage rolls. Coconut cream. Brandy snaps. Walnut whips. Iced cake. Chocolate fingers. Even a cucumber sandwich would have been something.

As they kissed us goodbye the air was full of their lovely scent. We waved goodbye, then walked back slowly.

'The rotten things,' my best friend said. 'The greedy, rotten things.'

The Teacher Trap

Martin Waddell

'Here it is!' said Harriet, plonking the Fruit Salad Anthea bowl on the end of the table in the Gym, where P7's Grand Feast was laid out.

P7 gathered round.

'What is it?' asked Fat Olga, standing well back from the placid green mixture in the bowl.

'It's a fruit salad!' said Anthea. 'Named after me.'

'Because she's my best friend,' said Harriet.

Anthea beamed proudly round at the rest of P7 who hadn't had fruit salads named after them because they weren't Harriet's Best Friends.

'What's *in* it?' said Sylvester Wise, going to the nub of the problem as usual.

'Lots of things!' said Anthea. 'Lots of lovely lovely things to match lovely lovely me!'

Not everybody present thought that Anthea was lovely, but nobody said so.

'It's smoky green, sort of,' said Olga, and she

considered *sniffing*, but thought better of it. You never know where a sniff will get you.

'Jolly well done, Harriet!' said Sylvester.

Harriet looked at him suspiciously. She was right to be suspicious. There was bound to be something wrong when the Leader of the Anti-Harriet League said something nice to Harriet.

'Brilliant, Harriet!' said Fat Olga, taking her cue from her Leader.

'Very nice,' said Marky Brown.

'Smashing!' said Charlie Green.

'You all sick, or something?' said Harriet. 'You don't *look* sick. Not any sicker than usual, that is.'

'Not at all, Harriet,' said Sylvester. 'It is our new policy. "Be-Nice-to-Harriet!" '

'Why?' said Harriet.

'It's because they really *like* you, Harriet, I expect,' said Anthea.

There was a long silence.

'Quite right!' said Sylvester, lying through his teeth.

'Prove it!' said Harriet.

'I will!' said Sylvester, and he walked down the table and whipped the cover off the ham sandwiches.

'I've named my ham sandwiches after you!' said Sylvester. 'That proves it!'

Harriet frowned. She wasn't sure that she

liked having ham sandwiches named after her.

'And my apple tart!' said Fat Olga, showing Harriet the apple tart.

'And my swiss roll!' said Charlie Green.

'I would have named my jelly after you, but I sat on it on the bus!' said Marky Brown, but he showed Harriet the sign and some bits of sat-on jelly.

The sign said: Jelly: Harriet.

'Oh lovely!' said Anthea. 'Aren't you proud to have all those things named after you, Harriet?'

Harriet looked at the Ham Sandwiches Harriet and the Apple Tart Harriet and the Swiss Roll Harriet and the empty plate where the sat-on Jelly Harriet would have been, if it hadn't been jelly-sat.

'Hmmm,' she said.

and

'Uhuh!'

and

'This needs thinking about!'

Harriet went away to think about it in the boiler room.

'Got her!' said Sylvester Wise triumphantly.

'Wise!' boomed Mr Tiger. 'Wise! Here, boy!'

Sylvester was out by the bike shed, counting bike rides on Charlie Green's bicycle, as the Anti-Harriet League lived up to their obligation to their voters.

'Sir?' said Sylvester.

'Who made what, Wise?' said Mr Tiger, coming to the point as usual. He wasn't the Pride of Slow Street for nothing, and he had been sent to find out, following an Emergency Meeting of the Staff in Miss Grandston's Room.

'*What* what, sir?' said Sylvester.

'The foodstuffs in the Grand Feast, Wise!' barked Mr Tiger. 'Who prepared what?'

'Don't know, sir,' said Sylvester innocently.

'Of course you know, boy!' said Mr Tiger. 'You're not foolish enough to eat anything made by Harriet, are you? Not after last year! The Staff *demand* to know what Harriet made, so that we can steer clear of it.'

'I couldn't say, sir,' said Sylvester.

Mr Tiger took a deep breath. 'There will no doubt be some particular foodstuff that you will *not* be touching, Wise?' he said, with tiger-like cunning.

'Oh yes, sir,' said Sylvester. 'The apple tart, sir. I wouldn't touch *that*, sir, not for anything!'

'Aah!' breathed Mr Tiger. 'Good boy, Wise! A wink is as good as a nod! Splendid little chap!'

And he rushed off to tell the Staff.

'What's wrong with my apple tart then?' said Fat Olga, coming up to Sylvester.

'Nothing,' said Sylvester.

'You told him you would be steering clear of the apple tart!' said Fat Olga.

'I'm allergic to apples,' said Sylvester.

'No you're not!' said Marky. 'You have one every breaktime!'

'I am *today*,' said Sylvester.

'I don't understand,' said Fat Olga.

'I didn't think you would,' said Sylvester. 'It's all part of my plan.'

'What plan?' said Olga.

'My Teacher Trap!' said Sylvester.

'No apple tart, anybody!' said Mr Tiger, marshalling the Staff.

'No apple tart!' the Staff chorused.

'And no ham sandwiches or swiss roll either!'

79

said Miss Granston.

'Why not?' said Mr Tiger.

'Because I've spied out the land!' said Miss Granston. 'They've got Harriet's name on!'

'Aaaaaaaah!' moaned the Staff.

And Miss Granston led them down the corridor toward the P7 Grand Feast with a proud beam of achievement on her face, little knowing what was to come.

'Anthea!' said Harriet. '*Look*, Anthea!'

'What, Harriet?' said Anthea, who was busy stuffing herself with little sausages on sticks, because she liked little sausages on sticks.

'My fruit salad!' said Harriet.

'*My* fruit salad, you mean,' said Anthea. 'Fruit Salad Anthea!'

'Yes,' said Harriet. 'It's the most popular thing there is!'

Harriet was right.

The teachers had gathered in a cloud round Fruit Salad Anthea. For one thing, it was at the far end of the table from Apple Tart Harriet and Jam Roll Harriet and even Ham Sandwiches Harriet, which made it a safer place to be, and for another it was delicious.

So it should have been, with apples and oranges and pineapples and peaches and cherries and grapes and avocados and invigorating nonalcoholic nettle wine and elderberry and nutmeg and cherry, with half a bottle of raw artichokes on top. 'Delicious!' said Miss Tremloe, sipping from her spoon.

'Do have some more, Mr Tiger!' said Miss Granston, and she helped her right-hand man to a fourth serving.

'Spot on!' said Mr Cousins. 'I feel quite out of myself.'

'. . . Om . . . pom . . . pom!' giggled Miss Wilson.

'Really lovely concoction, Anthea!' said Mrs Whitten, spooning away. 'Do congratulate your mother . . .'

'It wasn't *my* mother, Miss,' said Anthea. 'It's just named after me. It was . . .'

But her voice was drowned out by the sound coming from the corner where Miss Ash, who had had one or two helpings too many of the delicious fruit salad, was showing Mrs Barton how to do a Two-Step.

'One-two-three, one-two-three!' cried Miss Ash, adding a step too many because she suddenly felt carefree and happy and generous.

'Music! We need music!' cried Miss Wilson, flinging her arms in the air, and beginning to twirl, a wild glow lighting up her cheeks.

Miss Tremloe, who taught music and movement, was not to be outdone. She grabbed her guitar and strummed.

It was a fierce strumming, a jungle beat, something to do with fruit juices and invigorating wine.

Miss Wilson whipped off her shoes and grabbed Mr Cousins, who thought his lucky day had come.

They waltzed around the floor. Mr Tiger, caught up in the spirit of the thing, abandoned his pipe and his fourth helping of fruit salad and grabbed Miss Granston by the elbow. Off they clipped, to a Military Two-Step.

Mrs Barton did a Fandango with Mrs Whitten, followed by a strange and exotic dance she had once seen in a night club in Benidorm on a blind date. Hair was let loose, legs and arms flew. All the teachers were dancing and singing and bopping about to the throb of Miss Tremloe's unchained guitar.

'OOOOOH!' said Olga.

'Mission accomplished!' said Sylvester, with great satisfaction.

'They're all . . .' began Charlie Green, but he didn't get finished, because Mrs Barton grabbed him by the wrist, and whirled him into the dance.

It was then that Miss Wilson sat down on the floor.

She did it suddenly, because she had been

83

showing Mr Cousins what the Leading Swan did in Act Three of 'Swan Lake', and somehow the swan legs had done a wobble.

'Oooooh!' moaned Miss Wilson.

CRASH! Mr Tiger and Miss Granston fell over her.

BANG! Mrs Barton followed suit.

WALLOP!

The wallop was Mrs Whitten, who had retreated to a stool but fell off it just the same, bringing an abrupt end to Mrs Barton's dance.

All the teachers lay on the floor.

None of them stirred.

The P1s and P2s and P3s and P4s and P5s and P6s stood very still, and looked frightened.

The P7s cheered!

And that was when Sylvester Wise showed his true leadership qualities again.

'Silence, everyone!' he cried. 'Do not disturb our sleeping teachers! All Junior Classes will return to their rooms, collect their coats and bags and fly away home!'

Everybody cleared off, except the P7s.

'What about us?' said Charlie.

'We've still got the apple tart and the swiss roll and the ham sandwiches to finish,' said Sylvester. 'Nobody touched them!'

'You did that deliberately, Sylvester Wise!' said Harriet.

'Did what?' said Sylvester, tucking into the feast.

'You fixed it so the teachers would all stick to my fruit salad,' said Harriet.

'Didn't you want them to take it?' said Sylvester.

'Yes, but not so *much* of it,' said Harriet, who was beginning to wonder about the effects of nonalcoholic nettle wine and elderberry and nutmeg and cherry, with half a bottle of artichoke, all mixed in with fruit.

'They're all laid out on the floor, Harriet,' said Anthea.

'And that's where we're leaving them!' said Sylvester. 'It was *your* fruit salad, you can sort it out with them, when they come round!'

The rest of P7 cleared off, leaving Harriet and Anthea and a pile of teachers in the middle of the floor.

'I think . . . I think we're in trouble again, Harriet,' said Anthea unhappily.

Acknowledgements

The compiler and publishers wish to thank the following for permission to use copyright material in this anthology:

Lance Salway for 'The Boy Who Wasn't Bad Enough'.

Abelard-Schuman for 'Playing With Cuthbert' by René Goscinny from *Nicholas and the Gang*.

Viking Kestrel for 'The Crooked Little Finger' by Philippa Pearce from *Lion at School*.

Penguin Books Australia Limited for 'Licked' by Paul Jennings from *Unbearable*.

Faber & Faber for 'The Incredible Henry McHugh' by Robert Fisher from *Funny Folk*.

Viking for 'Horrible Harry and the Deadly Fish Tank' by Suzy Kline from *Horrible Harry and the Ant Invasion*.

Hamish Hamilton for 'Holiday With the Fiend' by Sheila Lavelle from *Holiday With the Fiend*.

Helen Cresswell for 'Snake in the Grass' from *Baker's Dozen*.

Mrs Ruth Jackson for 'Jelly Jake and Butter Bill' by Leroy F Jackson from *The Peter Patter Book*.

Andersen Press for 'When I Lived Down Cuckoo Lane and Lost a Fox Fur, and a Lot More Besides' by Jean Wills from *When I Lived Down Cuckoo Lane*.

Blackie and Co. for 'The Teacher Trap' by Martin Waddell from *Harriet and the Flying Teachers*.

COOL SCHOOL STORIES
0 09 926585 0   £4.99

MORE COOL SCHOOL STORIES
0 09 940023 5   £4.99

THREE IN ONE ANIMAL STORIES
0 09 926583 4   £4.99

COMPLETELY WILD STORIES
0 09 926584 2   £4.99

THREE IN ONE BALLET STORIES
0 09 926582 6   £4.99

THREE IN ONE PONY STORIES
0 09 940003 0   £4.99

MAGICAL MYSTERY STORIES
0 09 940262 9   £4.99

THE CHARLIE MOON COLLECTION
0 09 961221 6   £4.99

DOCTOR DOLITTLE STORIES
0 09 926593 1   £4.99

THE WILLARD PRICE ADVENTURE COLLECTION
0 09 926592 3   £4.99